Table of Contents

Introduction. 5

Chapter 1. 10

Chapter 2. 14

Chapter 3. 20

Chapter 4 Vivendi, June 2012. Asset Reproduction and Sum of the Parts Valuations. Spin offs and Asset Sales. 27

Chapter 5 L.B. Foster, July 2012. EBIT and Net Cash Valuation, EV/EBIT, Site and Book Recommendation. 45

Chapter 6 Altria, August 2012. Free Cash Flow and Revenue and EBIT Valuations. Debt, Pensions, Interest Rates, Litigation, Competitive Advantages, Off Balance Sheet Commitments, Site and Book Recommendation. 63

Chapter 7 Jack in the Box, October 2012. Price to Book and Tangible Book Valuation. Why You Must Do Your Own Research, Hype, Comparison to Competition, Catalysts, and Site Recommendation. 92

Chapter 8 Second Dole Valuation, November 2012. How to Value Land, Property, and Equipment, Combining Two Valuations Together, and Management Issues. 121

Chapter 9 Wendy's, November 2012. TEV/EBIT, Relative Valuations, Management Issues, Cap Ex, Share Buybacks, Contrarian, Negative Equity, and Book Values. 137

Chapter 10 Brazil Fast Food Company, December 2012. How To Calculate ROIC, Great Management, Competitive Advantages, Net Operating Loss Carryforwards (NOL's), Relative Valuations, OTC, and Pink Sheet Companies. 166

Chapter 11 Unico American Corporation, January 2013. Insurance Company Different Terms, Techniques, and Valuations, Float, Leveraged ROA, Site Recommendations, Negative EV, EV/EBIT, and TEV/EBIT. 204

Chapter 12 Bab Inc, March 2013. Incorporating NOL's Into Valuations, Relative Valuations, Management Issues, Excessive Compensation, Customer Reviews, and Overpriced Products. 234

Chapter 13 Paradise Inc, March 2013. Finding The Value of Land, Property, and Equipment, Hidden Assets, Cash Conversion Cycle, Small Niches, Moats, and Relative Valuations. 252

Chapter 14 Bab Inc Versus Paradise Inc Conclusion, March 2013. Margin Comparison, Earnings Yield, Making Tough Decisions, Cash Conversion Cycle, and Protection of Downside. 269

Chapter 15 Conclusion: Challenge To You, How I Do Research, Mindset, Patience, Character and Personality Traits of Value Investors, and When To Sell a Company. 292

Epilogue 318

Copyright

© 2013 Jason Rivera

Dedication

For my wife, kids, and family. Thank you for being there over the years and supporting me through everything. I would not have been able to do this without you.

Acknowledgements

"If I have seen a little further it is by standing on the shoulders of Giants." Sir Isaac Newton

Thank you to John from CSInvesting, Red from The Red Corner Blog, Taylor From Valueprax, Jeff, from Ragnar Is A Pirate, John from Shadowstock, The Brooklyn Investor, The Fundoo Professor, and all other value investing and related blogs for sharing your knowledge, conversations, and encouragements over the years. You all have had an extraordinary impact on my life and me as an investor and I would not be where I am today without all of you. Thank you so much.

Thank you to Dr. Wes Gray and Tobias Carlisle, authors of Quantitative Value, for your feedback and encouragements. This book is infinitely better because of the feedback from you both.

Thank you to Benjamin Graham, Warren Buffett, Seth Klarman, and Joel Greenblatt for sharing your experience and wisdom with the world.

Thank you to Tim Ferriss for sharing how to hack the world and sharing your adventures. Without the Four Hour Work Week and the sharing of your amazing life adventures I would have never had the motivation to finish writing this book.

Thank you to Dean and Eda Nelson, Chen Vincent, and Kevin McKenna for believing in the book enough to preorder it.

Introduction

"All intelligent investing is value investing--to acquire more than you are paying for. Investing is where you find a few good companies and then sit on your ass." Charlie Munger

I originally started my value investing blog, Value Investing Journey, and now this book, because I was frustrated that I could not find any other single site, group of sites, or books that talked about the things are in this book. Most value investing blogs will talk about the companies they think are good investments, show some basic valuations, talk about why they think the particular company is a good investment, and go into some detail about the company's operations. This approach is fine if you already know how to value and evaluate companies. If you do not however you are in for a very long, often times frustrating journey, through the infinite internet until you are finally able to piece enough disparate information together to start the process of learning and implementing valuation techniques, thought processes, and how to properly gauge whether a company is a potentially good investment into your own repertoire.

When the Value Investing Journey blog was started it was to keep a journal of my thoughts and valuation and analysis articles so that I could see what I was learning, how fast I was learning, and as a way to see how far I had come in the time since the blog was started. There was one other major reason it was begun and why this book was written. I wanted to help newer to intermediate level investors who like me could not, or did not, want to go to a big time university to learn the techniques that will be shown and talked about in this book so that you could jump-start your own investing journey a lot faster than the nearly 5 years it has taken me to gain the knowledge that I have. Throughout this book, and on the accompanying blog, I will show you and give you access to all the best information I have learned from, that took me thousands of hours to put together. You will be shown how to do the valuation techniques for yourself, talk about my investment thought processes and why I did what I did, and you will be given all the tools and necessary information so that you can also become an excellent investor without going to college and without having to spend potentially tens or hundreds of thousands of dollars. With this book and the accompanying blog you will not only be saving potentially hundreds of thousands of dollars on tuition costs, but you will also save potentially thousands of hours of time as well.

The premise of this book is very simple: You no longer need to go to an expensive Ivy League level school to learn how to become an excellent investor, and you will be shown the steps I took to teach myself about investing to become an excellent value investor. Almost 100% of the information that was learned was found free online but supplemented with books which is where the minimal costs came from. Since I have dealt with extreme dizziness since I was a senior in high school, I am now 26, and have not been able to go to college and do the typical Bachelor's degree in finance coupled with an MBA, finding a mentor and working for an investment firm of some kind. All of the learning I have done was on my own through the internet and its various websites, blogs, articles, newsletters, and books that were found or recommended where the disparate pieces were very slowly put together. This book will boil down all the important information that has taken me years to learn and if you have the right mind-set and drive to learn and practice the techniques and processes that will be shown than you too can become an excellent value investor.

The main reason it took me so long to learn the processes that will be shown throughout this book are because I have never been able to find one or even a few resources to learn from that taught all the techniques that will be shown in this book. One site may talk about the basics of investing but stops there, the next may show you advanced techniques that make no sense to you and could be written in Chinese for all you know since it is just a confusing blob of information, another site may show you basic valuation techniques but not what they mean or how to learn how to do them yourself, and the list goes on all the while eating into your precious time. This lead to frustrations and monetary loss either through losing money in the market like I did or delaying you from making money in the market because you are not confident in what you are doing.

It has taken me nearly five years reading thousands of books, articles, blogs, etc, probably tens or hundreds of thousands of pages of information, and thousands of hours practicing to get to the point where I am and feel like a lot of that time was wasted on stuff that didn't really matter in the grand scheme of things about how to evaluate a company. The reason I am writing this book because I want to help newer to intermediate level investors save potentially years of time by teaching you how to properly evaluate a company's prospects by reading its financial reports and any other information you can find online about the company, its management, competitors, and industry. Along with showing you the steps I took to learn what I have, you will also be shown various valuation techniques, taught how do to them, learn what they mean for the overall investment thesis, and be shown how to adjust the numbers so that you can cater them to your particular needs since every investors mind-set and needs are different. It took me a while to learn how important valuation is in terms of knowing whether a company is a good one to invest in at the time. Valuation is of utmost importance not only so that you do not buy into a company that is overvalued but also because it will let you decide what a company is worth so you can determine what a proper margin of safety is so that you can buy underneath that price. This is necessary because if you do make a mistake in your valuation or analysis you will still have a chance to make money by buying into said company at a substantial discount to it estimated intrinsic value. I will show you how to do this and much more by showing you real life valuation and analysis articles that I have written where you will be shown the thought process that I had while evaluating the company and how I came to my conclusions.

Like the premise of this book the structure of it is very simple and straight to the point as well. The first two chapters of this book are an introduction where I will talk about what originally got me interested in investing, how I started, some of the challenges I have had to overcome in the intervening years, and what finally got me to become serious about learning about investing. I will also detail some of the many mistakes I made early on to warn you and hopefully save you the investment money and time that was lost. Chapter three will tell you about my investment philosophy so that you can get an idea of where I am coming from when I talk about why I thought certain things while evaluating a company and my overall thought process. The rest of the book will be showing you the valuation and analysis articles, explain how to do everything, show you where the techniques were learned from and pointing you to those sources so that you can learn from them if you want deeper knowledge on the techniques.

If you want to become an excellent investor faster by spending less than continue on and learn from my value investing journey where I will show you how you too can become an excellent investor without having to go to college.

Chapter 1

"If your goal is to beat the market, an MBA or a Ph.D. from a top business school will be of virtually no help." Joel Greenblatt

I have always liked the thought of investing since learning the very basics of it and the power of compound interest during my senior year of high school in 2004/2005. At my high school every senior had to take one semester of government and one semester of consumerism; a kind of hybrid class that taught about a lot of different subjects one of them being the basics of investing. The power of compound interest which I did not fully understand at the time, and probably still do not understand fully, was one of the main things taught during the investing portions of that class along with basic investing ratios, what dividends were, and other very basic investing concepts. At the end of the class for the semester there was a project where we got put into groups of three or four people and found companies to invest in and invested money in those companies in a fake money account online. The group whose portfolio went up the most in the few week experiment won the contest and got the highest grade for that particular project.

I ended up being the leader of my particular group mainly because I was the only one who was very interested in the concept of investing in companies and the others in my group showed almost no interest in stocks or investing in general and just seemed to want our senior year to get over with as soon as possible while doing as little work as possible. The first batch of companies we picked were ones that typical hormone fueled teenage boys might pick to buy into (Playboy, Nike, etc.) I do not remember picking those particular companies for any reason other than we liked the products as they pertained to Nike, and thought that it would be cool to be Hugh Hefner and own Playboy (For the articles of course). This was the depth of our analysis on the first batch of companies that our group bought into. As the weeks went on and the school year got closer to ending, being normal seniors, the other members of the groups' interest dropped even further to becoming almost nonexistent and I was the only one still doing work on the project as the semester was getting ready to end.

Since I was pretty much left to my own devices, at that point I decided to start actually doing minimal research on a company that would be a fantastic investment not only for the class project but over the long term. The company was overtaking its competitors very quickly, it had its IPO within a year or two of that time frame, and was quickly becoming one of the most used and well known sites in the world. Again, this was the depth of the analysis at that time. Even then with my very limited knowledge I recognized without even knowing it what later I would call and look for in companies, a sustainable competitive advantage, or moat that made the company very attractive to own and something that a lot of investors look for when buying companies. Since I was, and still am, extremely competitive and wanted to win the contest, I dumped all of the other stocks in the portfolio that we bought just because they were cool and put the entire fake money portfolio into buying stock in this one company that was valued somewhere between $60-$70 a share if memory serves me right.

The company's stock did not end up going up enough for our group to win the contest but I was proven right over the long-term as the company that the entire fake money portfolio was put into, $100,000, was selling for between $60-$70 a share at that time. If I would have held those 1428-1666 shares of stock until this present writing with the company now selling for around $793 a share I would have turned that original 100K fake investment into between $1,132,404-$1,321,138 in eight years. That comes out to a compound annual growth rate (CAGR) of between 35.44% and 38.08% respectively. As an example of how phenomenal that is Warren Buffet, widely regarded as the best investor ever, has averaged a CAGR of 20% over 40 years so the potential gains would have been incredible.

This potential result while phenomenal was almost completely luck due to the lack of any kind of in-depth research and analysis on my part but it did teach me one very valuable lesson that I still adhere to today. If you buy stock into a company that has huge market share and a sustainable competitive advantage, over time you will do very well in investing. Combine that with other factors such as the company's margins, its competitors, industry and making sure a company is either undervalued by a substantial margin or fairly valued, and the results can be fantastic.

For those who have not guess the company that we would have made a killing on if it was a real money portfolio, it is the worldwide search engine leader, one of the biggest and most innovative companies in the world, Google, stock ticker (GOOG.)

Thus my first lessons in competitive advantage, market share, compound interest, and opportunity cost left an indelible mark on as I still vividly remember those lessons to this day and helped to kick-start my value investing journey.

Chapter 2

"Why do we fall? So we can learn to pick ourselves up."
Thomas Wayne, Batman Begins.

During my senior year of high school I also started getting dizzy spells often that made me nauseous and dizzy to the point where I could only lay down and watch TV until the feeling went away. This problem, which still persists to this day, only got worse over time and for the better part of three or four years after graduating high school all I could really do was lie around and watch TV. Luckily I found some doctors, physical therapists, and others who have somewhat figured out my problem and I have been slowly……..very slowly, getting better since around 2007 or 2008. During this whole time I have only been able to work at a paying job for around three month's total over nearly 10 years.

In 2009 we found out that my wife was pregnant with our first child which left me a bit stunned and made me scramble to figure out something I could do while still dealing with my dizziness all day every day that I could eventually make money at. The three things I came up with at that time were getting involved in local politics but I figured the world didn't need any more scum bag politicians. I thought about becoming a writer but at that time didn't really have any passion for writing and remember being told by one of my teachers in high school that "Hopefully you never want to become a writer because you are really bad at it." She was right as I was absolutely awful at that time, even worse than now if you can imagine that. The only other thing I came up with at the time was remembering how much I liked learning about stocks and the stock market when I was in high school. I finally decided to go down the path towards learning about investing not necessarily because I was excited about it but because out of the ideas I came up with it was the only one I even remotely liked.

By this time I had completely forgotten everything learned in consumerism class in high school other than how amazing compound interest is and the money I could have made if I would have invested real money in Google. Armed with this exciting and depressing memory of what could have been with Google, I started relearning the basics by reading book after book and any website I could find that looked like it had decent information. Slowly after gaining what I thought was enough knowledge (Looking back I am appalled that I started investing real money with the very limited amount of knowledge then) I started investing REAL money in companies who had good-looking ratios. Sadly to say that was pretty much my only basis of research before buying into a company at that time. I was not even looking at balance sheets, cash flows, reading annual or quarterly reports, no valuations of any kind, and only did very minor research into what the company even did for business, YIKES!

This begins the first lessons that you can learn:

1) When you think you know enough about investing to start using real money stop yourself and invest in a fake money portfolio, watch your returns for a while and learn from your mistakes so you do not lose real money like I did.

2) If you are going to be serious about investing you need to read at the very least: The company's most recent annual report called a 10K, the company's most recent quarterly report called a 10Q, and the company's most recent proxy report which outlines things likes how much management gets paid and how they get paid, how much certain companies and people own of the company including company insiders, and if there are any family or related party transactions. I would actually recommend reading AT LEAST five years (I generally read at least 10 years worth of annual reports now) worth of annual reports, but starting with one year is better than nothing.

3) DO NOT invest in a company just because it has "good looking ratios" or because you have heard that the company is about to come out with a fantastic product, or that the company has amazing future potential, etc. This is almost all hype and usually does not end up coming to fruition and you will most likely lose money if you invest off of hype like the previous examples. Do your own in-depth research and invest in companies that way or you will get punished like I did.

Mr. Market, Benjamin Graham's term for describing the stock market, saw that I was making a mockery of him by only investing real money with minimal knowledge and decided to punish me for it. Because I only invested in companies that had good-looking ratios, a good chunk of my portfolio was in Chinese small caps and shortly after starting to invest in them rumblings started coming from all directions that a lot of these companies were nonexistent in some cases, their financial statements were not accurate, and that some were outright lying to customers and shareholders. Various other problems also started to come out about Chinese small caps shortly after I decided in my infinite wisdom to put half of my portfolio into these small Chinese companies. The continuous bad news led people to flee these stocks leaving me with around a 50% decline in my portfolio in a matter of months after starting real money investing. Luckily I was smart enough to only invest a small amount of money at that time so the absolute loss ended up being only about $500 but it still stings and embarrasses me to this day how naïve I was then.

After this happened I took a breath and reevaluated what I was doing and what I wanted to accomplish through investing. What I was doing then was not actually what I would consider investing now. What I was doing then I consider speculation, akin to gambling, since I was doing only minimal research into companies before deciding to buy into them and which is a big no-no if you want to truly become a better investor. I had a realization at that point that if I wanted to get serious about becoming a true investor and stop losing money that I needed to dedicate myself to the craft, cut out outside distractions, and actually learn how to evaluate and value companies properly before deciding to buy into them. I either needed to do this or stop investing completely because if I kept doing what I was doing I would have ended up losing a lot more money.

Sometime around then I found John Chew's amazing site, now csinvesting.org, which at least partly saved my investing and my family's financial future. Through his site I learned a lot and still learn a lot about how to evaluate and value companies and owe a good part of what I know and have become as an investor to him and his site and would highly recommend it to anyone who wants to become a better investor. Shortly after finding his site and taking Aswath Damodaran's free online course on how to value companies, which I would also recommend, I decided to completely dedicate myself to becoming a true value investor and set myself on that path.

However, even with his wonderful site and the hundreds or thousands of other sites, books, blogs, articles, etc that I have read, specific information that was sought was still too far spread out in my opinion and I have not been able to find one book or site that encompasses even close to everything that I will share throughout this book. It has taken me almost five years to get to the point where I am at now and I think I can help you save months or years of time by teaching you specifics on how to evaluate and value companies.

There is no one right way to do things and I will be showing you the ways that make the most sense to me. The best thing I can recommend to anyone who wants to become a better investor is that as soon as you get comfortable with the concepts and terms that will be shown in this book is that you should go and start reading annual and quarterly reports for public companies and start practicing the techniques and start taking notes on the companies you are researching so that you can evaluate and value the company for yourself. I can only help to show you the way to becoming a better investor but you have to walk down the path yourself.

Chapter 3

"Nothing in the world can take the place of Persistence. Talent will not; nothing is more common than unsuccessful men with talent. Genius will not; unrewarded genius is almost a proverb. Education will not; the world is full of educated derelicts. Persistence and determination alone are omnipotent. The slogan 'Press On' has solved and always will solve the problems of the human race." Calvin Coolidge

Throughout the rest of the book you will be seeing my actual analysis and evaluation articles where that will show you the valuations and analysis that I have done on real world companies. You will be shown how to value companies using various valuation techniques and how to adjust the numbers for yourself, and what those numbers and valuations mean for the overall investment thesis. You will also be shown my reasoning's and thought processes for why I decided what I did and why the particular company was a buy or sell decision for me at that particular point. Before we get to that though I need to state my investing philosophy so that everyone knows what frame of mind I am approaching the analysis with.

I look for companies that have some combination of the following criteria: Some kind of long-term sustainable competitive advantage, or moat as it is also called, companies that produce and sell products in niche markets, companies that I find to be substantially undervalued, have very good management, high insider ownership, are fantastically profitable, have a lot of cash and/or hidden assets, etc.

I only take into consideration in the valuations and analysis what I can see now, and pay almost no attention to rumoured future possibilities or estimates of revenues and margins into the future. The only time future possibilities play even a small role in my articles are in situations where there is a clear catalyst: Activist/value investing firm or individual involved, the company is undergoing a strategic review and is owned and controlled by a few people as in the case with Dole (DOLE) that you will see later in the book, or the company's management is trying to figure out ways to unlock the companies undervaluation by asset sales or spin offs as in the situation with Vivendi (VIVHY.PK) that you will see later in the book. Even with the above mentioned companies I only valued and analysed the company as it stood then, and treated future potential as icing on the cake that played almost a zero role in the evaluations.

My number one rule when I buy into a company is preserving capital and making sure that I do not lose money. The fewer losses I have, the more money that is kept and is able to compound faster when I do find winners so I am a very strict, disciplined, and conservative value investor. I generally only buy into companies that are selling at a substantial discount, or margin of safety, to my estimate of value for the company so that this way if I do make a mistake in the analysis or valuations then I will still have a chance to make some money. I usually look for a catalyst that could help unlock the undervaluation of a company such as: Potential for spin-off or asset sale, land or buildings that are not being used that could be sold, activist funds/investment firms that own stock in the company and could push for changes to be made, etc. I try to find areas of the market where a lot of investors do not or cannot invest and I generally only research companies that have market caps of less than $100 million or special situations like spin offs. Now that I am more confident in my abilities to value and evaluate companies I do not hesitate to put 20+ percent of my portfolio into one or more companies. The fewer companies I own the better I know each company. I am also a very contrarian investor and try to find companies that are either unknown, unloved, or are having problems for potential investments as well. The less competition there is the better when looking for investments so I try to steer clear of the herd who generally concentrate on bigger companies. I do not forecast numbers years or even months in advance at all and only value and analyze what I see in the company now so you will not see any DCF valuations in this book. There are a lot of books out there that explain how to do DCF valuations and I would highly recommend Aswath Damodaran's free online course on valuation where he teaches how to do DCF valuations if you are interested in those kinds of valuation techniques.

I generally plan to hold the companies I buy for years, decades, or hopefully forever if it turns out to be an exceptionally good company and generally only plan to sell if the companies if their share price rises to the high-end of my valuation range quickly or far above what I think its intrinsic value is after I have bought into it, or if I can find another company that I think is a better investment.

Having stated all of this you now have a frame-work for my thought process going forward and how I manage my personal portfolio and the other portfolios that I manage. If you come across any terms that you do not know refer to investopedia.com as it is the best site I have found that explains investing terms and it is still a site I use to this day when coming across things I do not know or understand. If you do not find a definition that you find satisfactory or just want to study something further you should search for the term, person, book, etc on my blog or through Google.

I would also like to mention that I have received no formal training in evaluating companies and some of the ratios that will be talked about throughout the book I came up with on my own and have never seen used anywhere else such as the total obligations, commitments, and debt/EBIT ratio which will be talked about later. I am sure that some professional investors and college professors out there will say that I am technically probably not doing some of the things in this book properly or "How they should be done" but since I had to learn on my own, I have learned to do things that make sense to me, help me to understand the inner workings of a company, and help me to make an informed decision about whether or not a company is a good investment. In my opinion understanding these things in your own particular way, which makes sense to you, is more important than doing things just because someone else says they are proper. If something in this book doesn't make sense to you, don't use it, find your own way to make sense of things, and come back to it later. This book is meant to be a practical guide of learning how to evaluate and decide if a company is a good investment without having to spend potentially hundreds of thousands of dollars on a college degree. Use what makes sense to you, skip the rest, and come back to it later when it does make sense to you and you want to learn how to use it.

One piece of advice before we get to chapters about technique and analysis is that at the beginning of each chapter I will state which company I am valuing and analysing. If you want to get the most out of this book once you get comfortable with the terms and techniques you should stop reading after finding out the company and time period the evaluations were done and go online to Morningstar.com or the company's website and download the annual, quarterly, and proxy reports from the time period mentioned. If you are a new investor I would recommend starting at the beginning of the book and go chapter by chapter because the book is structured to start slow with easier concepts and a lot less information. I then build up to harder to understand concepts as it can be very easy to get overwhelmed by some of the later chapters if you are just starting out. I also built this book with more advanced investors in mind who only want to learn about certain specific techniques. In the title of each chapter you will be shown which company the chapter is about, the stock ticker in parenthesis, the time period the company was researched, and what will be talked about in the chapter so you can go back and read those financial reports and skip to specific chapters if you want to learn a specific technique.

I highly recommend reading though the chapters, writing down some of your own notes, thoughts and valuations and then come back and read the analysis, valuations, and my thought and decision-making process to see if we came to different conclusions. This is a very good way to practice the techniques that you will be shown and will help you retain more information faster. We may come to similar conclusions or we may not, and just because we may come to different conclusions does not mean either of us is wrong. As long as you put thought into your analysis, do the research, and come to logical, unemotional decisions only Mr. Market can decide after a few years whom is right or wrong. Learning a sound investment process that makes sense to you and leads you to logical, unemotional investing decisions should be very high on your priority list because if you do develop those traits you will generally do well investing over time. Anyone can learn the techniques and terms in this book, not everyone can develop or have the proper investment thought processes and other traits that will be talked about later to become an excellent value investor. If you can come up with a very sound investment process then you will already be far ahead of most MBA's and professional investors who generally invest with the herd and let their emotions take control of their decision-making process.

For the rest of this book you will be shown real life valuation and analysis that I have put together on companies. For further insights and to learn from people who have commented on some of my research I have listed ways below to view the original articles and the comments and discussion they have garnered. Some of the comments on my articles have had very valuable information in them that I have learned from and would highly recommend going to the following sites for further discussion. You can go to the following pages and search for the specific articles which will have the comments at the bottom of the pages.

- My Blog-Value Investing Journey
- Seeking Alpha author page: **http://seekingalpha.com/author/jason-rivera/articles**
- Guru Focus author page: **http://www.gurufocus.com/news.php?author=Jason+Rivera**

Chapter 4 Vivendi (VIVHY.PK) June 2012. Asset Reproduction and Sum of the Parts Valuations. Spin offs, Asset Sales.

"The important thing is not to stop questioning. Curiosity has its own reason for existing. One cannot help but be in awe when he contemplates the mysteries of eternity, of life, of the marvelous structure of reality. It is enough if one tries merely to comprehend a little of this mystery every day. Never lose a holy curiosity." Albert Einstein

- **Vivendi**

    Vivendi (VIVHY.PK) combines the world leader in video games (Activision Blizzard ATVI), the world leader in music (Universal Music Group), the French leader in alternative telecommunications (SFR), the Moroccan leader in telecoms (Maroc Telecom), the leading alternative broadband operator in Brazil (GVT), and the French leader in pay-TV (Canal+ Group). The previous information was taken from

Vivendi's website. I will get to further descriptions of the subsidiaries later.

For a discussion of the unsponsored Vivendi ADR, versus the foreign listing of Vivendi (VIVEF.PK), view the comments in http://seekingalpha.com/article/523121-vivendi-undervalued-french-media-and-telecom-conglomerate.

I have used two different valuation techniques for Vivendi. The first is an asset reproduction valuation done on 4-2-2012. All numbers are in millions of Euros unless otherwise noted, except the per share numbers. Valuations were done using 2011 10K.

Assets:	Book Value:	Reproduction Value
Current Assets		
Cash	3,304	3,304
Marketable Securities	1,544	1,544
Accounts Receivable (net)	6,730	4,500

Inventories	805	500
Prepaid Expenses	0	0
Deferred Taxes-Tax Liability	700	400
Total Current Assets	13,083	10,248
PP&E Net	9,001	6,000
Goodwill	25,029	12,514.50
Intangible Assets	6,814	3,407
Total Assets	53,927	32,169.50

- Number of shares is 1,242 million.

Reproduction value:

- With IA 32,169.5/1,242= 24.90 Euros per share = $34.24 per share

- Without IA 28,762.5/1,242= 23.16 Euros per share = $30.62 per share

Current share price on 4-21-2012 = $16.50 per share

Sum of the parts valuation done on 4-26-2012 all numbers in millions of Euros unless otherwise noted, except per share data.

- 44% of SFR bought in 2011 for 7,750 Euros. Implied value of total stake since Vivendi now owns 100% of SFR = 17,360 Euros
- 60% of Activision (ATVI) =6,587 Euros
- 100% of SFR + 60% of ATVI =23,947 Euros = $31,629 million

Vivendi has a total market cap currently of $23.46 billion

You are getting most of the 60% of ATVI, all of GVT, all of Canal+, all of UMG, 53% of Maroc Telecom, which equals 5.41 billion Euros, all cash and debt for free, just by purchasing part of ATVI and all of SFR. GVT, Canal+, UMG, and Maroc Telecom are the rest of their subsidiaries whose operations will be described later.

Valuing the whole of Vivendi, cash, and debt using my above estimates, I am estimating a very conservative 40 Billion Euros, which equals $53.832 billion of total value for Vivendi.

- $53.832 billion/number of shares at full dilution of 1.250 billion= $43.07 per share
- Current share price = $18.60 per share

This valuation would be used if it were to do a spin-off or selling some of its assets and companies.

The reproduction valuation is generally the most conservative intrinsic value estimate and the one I use the most since I am very conservative and want the biggest margin of safety as possible.

Some other things I like about Vivendi besides the massive margin of safety are: It pays a healthy yearly dividend, has consistent free cash flow of at least 3 billion Euros per year after cap ex, very good margins, cash and cash equivalents of over 3 billion Euros, and it also has net operating loss carry forwards of around 8 billion Euros.

Seth Klarman owns shares of Vivendi at his hedge fund Baupost Group, and has been buying more recently. I actually got lucky and bought shares of VIVHY at a cheaper price than Klarman. Also the management of Vivendi is reviewing what it could do to unlock the value that is missing right now, by its own estimates at least 40%.

Risks: A lot of debt and continual huge amounts of cap ex in the telecom subsidiaries. The continuing European debt issues, with most of its business being done in Europe, specifically France. If it decides not to do a spin-off or asset sale it could take a while to unlock value, which would not bother me since it would enable me to acquire more shares.

I would like it to eventually do some kind of spin-off or asset sale to pay down its debt, which should also increase the share price. I would not mind if it cancelled the dividend for a year or two to pay down debt either.

Description of subsidiaries:

Activision Blizzard description - World's biggest video game company, and in my opinion has the best overall portfolio of games in the entire industry. Call of Duty, Skylanders, Diablo, Starcraft, World of Warcraft, among others are included in the portfolio. This is the asset that I think would make the most sense to sell or spin off.

Call of Duty produces over $1 billion of revenue by itself with every game produced, which comes out once a year usually in November.

However, most of these franchises have either just come out with games or are past their prime in my opinion. World of Warcraft, while still a cash cow, is gushing subscription members every month, and Blizzard has already started to move resources into the next MMORPG, which has no release date. Diablo III just came out so I don't expect another game in that series for a while. Call of Duty, while still producing huge revenue and profits, is at its peak in my opinion and can only go down from here. The development studio that makes the Call of Duty series has also been fighting with and losing a lot of team members over the last several years, which will hurt quality in the future.

I also see the entire console video game industry in a decline as well. You can only keep asking people to pay more for less for so long before they decide to stop buying games and consoles, especially with cheaper games coming out either free to play or for under $10 on tablets and phones.

The next generation of gaming systems is going to start coming out later in 2012. That is generally a bad thing for game publishers because of higher development costs and lower profitability. Thus another reason it should sell before the new consoles start coming out.

In my opinion now would be the perfect time to sell ATVI. Vivendi will likely never be able to get a higher price than now due to the above. The only problem would be finding someone big enough to buy.

GVT description - A fixed phone line and internet telecom with operations in Brazil who Vivendi recently bought. GVT has great growth potential but will cost a lot in the short term due to high amounts of cap ex in the telecom industry. Should be one of the better Vivendi holdings over the long term though as the margins are currently very good. My main concern with this one is that Vivendi over paid for it so it will take longer to recoup the initial investment. Also being in Brazil, you never know what company might be expropriated by the governments in South America.

Maroc Telecom description (MAOTF.PK) - Maroc Telecom is a mobile/internet/fixed line phone company with most of its business in Morocco. It has the same problem with cap ex as GVT above, especially since it is going to be transitioning into 3G coverage from 2G. That could eventually pay off however due to more data plan subscriptions from the smart phones that will run 3G. Maroc has also been having problems with the government in Morocco as it has had to cut phone rates, thus losing out on revenue and lowering margins.

Canal+ description - A pay TV/cinema company with operations mainly in France. Canal+ is

another asset I could see the company spinning off or selling because it currently owns 80% of Canal+ France and has been trying to buy the remaining 20% to no avail, which could lead it to sell its portion of it. It does own the rights to show Ligue 1 soccer matches
and UEFA Champions League matches in France, which is a major advantage.

Universal Music Group description - Biggest owner of music and music publishing rights in the world. UMG produces the lowest EBITDA and CFFO margin of the entire group. Also doesn't seem to fit the profile of the rest of the subsidiaries, which might lead this to being sold. However, it owns the rights to music from the likes of: Rihanna, Lady Gaga, Justin Bieber, Eminem, Taylor Swift and various other major music artists. The music industry could also see a comeback to higher profitability with things like ITunes, Pandora and Spotify though if it can figure out how to monetize the publishing rights properly.

Description of SFR - A mobile/fixed phone/internet telecom with operations mostly in France. Currently Vivendi's biggest revenue generator and probably the most important to the group's success in the future. SFR is currently facing some headwinds in France, having to cut rates, which are lowering margins. SFR is also facing new, tougher and cheaper competition in its market, which is currently lowering margins and causing a loss of subscribers. It is also losing some business due to the difficulties of the European economy and the loss of discretionary income by some individuals. Vivendi recently bought out the remaining 44% of SFR from Vodafone, which in my opinion it overpaid for, but should hopefully pay off in the future when and if SFR's operations turn around.

Analysis Explanation

For the rest of this book every company's valuations and analysis chapters will be left to the most part intact from the period I originally wrote it with only minor grammatical, formatting, and editing changes made.

This is the first true valuation and analysis article that I published. Looking back now I would have done a few things differently (Add debt into the sum of the parts valuation, add in the net operating loss carry forwards, and some other things that we will talk about later) but overall this is a good starting point for this book. The entire thesis after evaluating Vivendi was that they were extremely undervalued, at least 40% by managements own estimates, and that there were potential short and medium term catalysts that could help unlock this undervaluation. The company was going through what is called a strategic review at the time where management was trying to figure out ways to improve the price of the company's stock and were talking about either doing a spinoff of one of its subsidiaries to current Vivendi shareholders, or outright selling one of the subsidiaries to a third-party. The reason for doing this was that Vivendi is hoping that it could use the proceeds from a spin-off or asset sale to pay off company debt, which was substantial at the time, to become a more focused and profitable company which would hopefully help raise the share price and in turn the perceived value of the company. Vivendi management was further incentivized to do a spin-off or asset sale of some kind because debt rating companies were threatening to downgrade the company's debt rating to just above junk level if it was not able to lower its substantial debt load. The lowering of an entities debt can be a very bad thing as this makes it harder for the company to raise debt, it makes it more expensive to raise debt, and it can raise the interest rate on the company's current outstanding debt which would lead to a further decrease in profitability due to higher interest and debt related costs.

The factors I talk about in the article, combined with the factors directly above and below led me to believe this company was a good buy. Management was incentivized to do some kind of spin-off or asset sale to raise cash and lower the company's debt, I was buying the company at a substantial discount to the intrinsic value that was calculated for the company, (buy price around $18 a share and a minimum estimate of value of $30 per share) all of which made this company a very good, safe buy at that time. In addition to the above factors my downside was covered by several very valuable and saleable assets; in this case other companies. Some of the subsidiaries are public companies so you could gauge how much they were worth in the open market in comparison to what the total of Vivendi was worth. As an example Activision Blizzard, which Vivendi owned 60% of at the time is a public company so I checked out what it was selling for by itself. ATVI at the time was selling as a whole in the stock market for around 9.222 billion Euros or about $12.15 billion just by itself. Vivendi owns 60% of ATVI which was worth at the time $7.29 billion and it had five other subsidiaries and cash that were not even counted. Vivendi's entire market cap at the time was around $23 billion meaning that just one of its subsidiaries, one of the smaller ones at that, covered about 32% of Vivendi's entire value. Remember that Vivendi still had five other subsidiaries to count, its cash, NOL's and the subtracting of debt as well.

Asset Reproduction Valuation

For an explanation of the asset reproduction valuation, the reasoning behind it, and how to adjust the numbers I highly recommend reading

Bruce Greenwald's Value Investing: From Graham to Buffett and Beyond. I learned from this book and other sources on how to adjust the numbers to get a realistic valuation but have adjusted some of the numbers further from what is recommended in the book and various other places I have learned from to meet my specific criteria, which will be explained below.

Cash, cash equivalents, short-term investments, and marketable securities: For the most part these are valued at 100% of book value. The only time I discount any of the above is if a company has operations in a foreign country and some of its money is in that foreign country. The reason I discount the cash and other above items in this case are because if the company wanted to repatriate this money back into the US it would have to pay taxes on this amount. Generally I estimate about a 40% tax rate on the portion of cash that would need to be repatriated.

Accounts Receivable Net: As a general rule I always use 85% of book value as my estimate of reproduction value. If the company needed to collect these in an emergency they could collect a pretty high portion of them if they needed to which is why I use a high estimate here.

Inventories: This is where the valuations start to get to be more art than science as what to discount this number and the ones that follow is highly subjective and dependant on what industry the company is in and how conservative of an investor you are. For example a clothing retailer who caters towards teenagers; their inventory may need to be discounted more because of how fast fashion and teenagers in general change their minds. Keep in mind for the rest of these calculations that I am an extremely conservative investor and that I want as safe a valuation as possible. I generally use about 60% of stated book value as my estimate of reproduction value for inventory. Some companies are higher, some are lower but I have found 60% is generally a pretty good estimate.

Prepaid expenses, tax assets, and other financial related assets: Again, this is highly dependent on the company and how they operate but I generally use between 40-60% of stated book value as my reproduction value estimate. As I will talk about in a later chapter these can be a very good source of float which can be a very desirable thing to find in a company.

Property, Plant, and Equipment-PP&E, net after depreciation: This one is also highly dependent on the industry but is easier to judge than some of the above amounts because you can generally find comparison values for these things. Generally I use around 50% of stated book value as my reproduction value estimate. Companies who are manufacturers and have old plants and equipment may need to be discounted by more than this amount. This number can also be deceiving though because if a company's PP&E has been fully depreciated then these assets come off the company's books completely. As an example a company like Dole (DOLE) who has owned some of its land in Hawaii for more than 100 years has a completely hidden asset that has been taken off the books due to depreciation that needs to be counted in the valuation and could be worth a lot of money. In the case of Dole, which will be talked about in a later chapter, potentially as much as $500 million in land value is either understated or completely off the company's books.

Goodwill: This is one term that needs to be very carefully learned and looked at when evaluating a company as it can be dangerous if counted on too much. This is a personal bias of mine but I generally do not like goodwill and generally take 50% and under of stated book value and use it as the estimate of reproduction value. In some cases I write this completely off when finding the reproduction value of a company as it is pretty much just an accounting number that has almost no effect on tangible assets. I highly recommend reading Professor Aswath Damodaran's many discussions on his blog about this subject to get a better idea of how this "asset" should be counted while doing valuations. Goodwill is considered an intangible asset and the following description should also be thought about when valuing goodwill as well.

Intangible assets: These are things like the value of patents, trademarks, and customer lists. I generally use 50% and under of this value stated at book as my estimate of reproduction value, again sometimes writing this off completely if it is warranted. The reason I discount these assets so much is that unless it is a long-term trademark or patent then generally these assets are not things that should be counted on for years or decades as a source of value for the company. For example how much value should a company's IA be worth in a pharmaceutical company that only makes one product that it has patented and exclusive rights to for a set amount of time, generally around 10 years. If the patent has just started it is probably fine to count all or most of the intangible assets when doing an asset reproduction valuation. But what if the patent is due to expire within 5 years and the company has no other products that are even close to coming on the market? What if the patent is expiring next year and the company's next product won't come out for 4 more years, would you want to count this whole amount in your valuation? As a conservative investor I wouldn't and generally don't like to count on things that are so-called intangible too much. This is why I generally exclude goodwill and IA from my asset reproduction valuations when dividing the total amount by the number of shares to find the per share value of the company.

Sum Of The Parts Valuation

This type of valuation is best used when evaluating a holding company or conglomerate that has a lot of subsidiaries as is the case with Vivendi or has a lot of land, buildings, and equipment that you can find approximate values for as in the case of Dole which we will get to later in the book. This valuation is one of the simplest valuations to understand but can take the longest to find all the numbers to use in the calculations. If a company is like Vivendi and has a few subsidiaries that are public companies you can just go to Morningstar or other financial sites to get the value of the company by looking at its market cap. If the company owns only a percentage of the company and not the whole thing just take the percentage of the company owned and take away that percentage of the market cap as I showed above with Vivendi's portion of Activision Blizzard. If the company owns a lot of land, buildings, and equipment, you will need to find exact or at least the best approximate values you can online. I will detail this in my chapter on Dole later and while this is still very straight forward this can be very time consuming but is necessary to do in these kind of cases because you may find a company who has a lot of so called hidden value as you will see later in the chapters about Dole and Paradise Inc.

Chapter 5: L.B. Foster (FSTR) July 2012. EBIT and Net Cash Valuation, EV/EBIT, Site And Book Recommendation.

"You miss 100% of the shots you don't take." Wayne Gretzky

L.B. Foster operates individual business units that specialize in rail, construction and tubular products. These groups manage manufacturing, distribution and sales facilities worldwide. The company also functions as a distributor and service provider in strategic alliances with industry leading manufacturing and engineering firms. They have three distinct business segments:

TUBULAR PRODUCTS

L.B. Foster Coated Products operates an ISO 9001:2008 Registered facility that applies FBE corrosion protection, ARO over coating and internal linings in an advanced technology environment. The coating plant is located on the site of American Steel Pipe's Birmingham, Alabama operations. L.B. Foster Threaded Products has the experience required to deliver quality water well products in today's rapidly changing environment. Our company has been a trusted supplier to the vertical pump industry for more than 30 years. The L.B. Foster team of professionals provides timely delivery, superior reliability, consistent quality and an ongoing commitment to customer satisfaction.

CONSTRUCTION PRODUCTS

L.B. Foster Piling has supplied flat, pipe, H beams and Z sheet pile to the construction industry for more than 80 years. L.B. Foster's long experience in the production and application of sheet piling extends to today's current line of quality sheet piling sections. A wide range of piling accessories, sheet piling and pipe piles are available nationally for sale or rent from convenient regional stocking locations. L.B. Foster Piling maintains a strategic relationship with Gerdau Long Steel North America and PND Engineers, Inc.

CXT Concrete Buildings is the leading U.S. manufacturer of precast concrete restroom, shower and concession buildings. These durable structures are in use at federal, state, county, city and private recreational sites. L.B. Foster Fabricated Bridge Products provides steel grid bridge flooring, bridge drainage systems, bridge railing, custom pedestrian railing and complete bridge solutions. L.B. Foster bridge products can be found on signature spans in North and South America.

RAIL PRODUCTS

The Rail Products group is a leading, one-source supplier and manufacturer of quality railroad products for mainline, transit, mining, port and industrial markets worldwide. Our full line of railroad products includes new rail, used rail, track work materials, rapid response/emergency track panels, crane rail, crane conductor systems, insulated rail joints, concrete ties, rail lubrication systems, transit rail systems, railway securement systems and locomotive and car repair equipment.

As of the 2011 10K the rail segment contributed 55% of revenues, the construction segment 40%, and the tubular segment 5%.

Descriptions of business segments above were taken from the 2011 10K.

Valuations were done using first quarter 2012 10Q and 2011 10K. All numbers are in millions of US dollars, except per share info, unless otherwise noted.

First valuation

Total Current Assets	230	175.1
PP&E Net	48	24
Goodwill	44	20
Intangible Assets Net	42.4	20
Investments	3.5	0
Other Assets	1.5	0
Total Assets	369.4	239.1

Total number of shares is 10.1

Reproduction Value:

- With Intangible assets: 239.1/10.1=$23.67 per share.

- Without Intangible assets: 219.1/10.1=$21.69 per share.

Current share price is $28.94 per share.

Second valuation

- Cash and cash equivalents of 67.8
- Total number of shares are 10.1
- Total current liabilities are 72

Short term investments + cash and cash equivalents- total current liabilities=

- 67.8+0-72=-4.2
- -4.2/10.1=-$0.42 in net cash per share.

L.B. Foster has and EBIT of 5.1-1+35=39.1. I am using the trailing twelve month EBIT number.

- 5X, 8X, 11X, and 14X EBIT+ cash and cash equivalents are:
- 5X39.1=195.5+67.8=263.3/10.1=$26.07 per share.
- 8X39.1=312.8+67.8=380.6/10.1=$37.68 per share.
- 11X39.1=430.1+67.8=497.9/10.1=$49.30 per share.
- 14X39.1=547.4+67.8=615.2/10.1=$60.91 per share.

Current share price is $28.94 per share.

- Market cap is 286.7 million.
- Enterprise value is 221.5 million.
- EV/EBIT= 221.5/39.1=5.67.

Since I am a very conservative investor I usually use the lowest estimate of value as my base case. Since the company has good margins, which I will get to shortly, I am going to be using the 8X EBIT estimate of value which is $37.68 per share as my base estimate of value.

With the current share price at $28.94 per share that gets us about a 25% margin of safety. Good, but not good enough, as I always want at the very least a 30% margin of safety. This company also has some other concerns which I will get to shortly but for now onto the positives.

- The company has had a current ratio of over 2 since 2006. A quick ratio of over 1.5 since 2007.
- Insiders own 5% of the company. I would like this to be a bit higher but it is good enough.
- They have been creating free cash flow since 2008.
- Return on equity since 2005 has been at least 7%.
- Return on invested capital has been at least 5% since 2005.
- The company has no current debt.
- They have available credit facilities of $123 million.
- Gross margins have been over 15% since 2007.
- Operating margin, or EBIT margin, has been over 5% since 2007.
- The company has recently started paying a dividend and the payout ratio is only 4%, which leaves room for growth.

- Book value per share has been steadily increasing over the years and the company is currently selling for about book value.
- The company is selling at a very low 5.67 EV/EBIT.

The Tubular and Rail segments have the best gross margins of the company at 29%, and 22% respectively. The construction gross margin is 14%, still very good.

With all of the above, FSTR sounds like a screaming buy when it gets to my 30% margin of safety right? Not so fast.

The company has some risks: pricing competition, poor economy, construction segment of the business is losing revenue due to the Federal Stimulus having run out the company's backlog of orders has also been decreasing recently. The backlog of orders is used to gauge, possible future revenue. With those concerns I would still probably be a buyer for sure, just needing a bit more margin of safety.

However, they do have one possibly gigantic concern that I have not talked about yet. They have an outstanding warranty claim against them that could be devastating to the company if it is found that they sold some defective concrete ties.

Quoting from its most recent 10Q.

- *Product Liability Claims-On July 12, 2011 the Union Pacific Railroad (UPRR) notified the Company and the Company's subsidiary, CXT Incorporated (CXT), of a warranty claim under CXT's 2005 supply contract relating to the sale of prestressed concrete railroad ties for the UPRR. The UPRR has asserted that a significant percentage of concrete ties manufactured in 2006 through 2010 at CXT's Grand Island, NE facility fail to meet contract specifications, have workmanship defects and are cracking and failing prematurely. Approximately 1.6 million ties were sold from Grand Island to the UPRR during the period the UPRR has claimed nonconformance. The 2005 contract calls for each concrete tie which fails to conform to the specifications or has a material defect in workmanship to be replaced with 1.5 new concrete ties, provided, that UPRR within five years of a concrete tie's production, notifies CXT of such failure to conform or such defect in workmanship.*
- *The UPRR's notice does not specify how many ties manufactured during this period are defective nor which specifications it claims were not met or the nature of the alleged workmanship defects. CXT believes it uses sound workmanship processes in the manufacture of concrete ties and has not agreed with the assertions in the UPRR's warranty claim notice. The UPRR has also notified CXT that ties have failed a certain test that is specified in the 2005 contract. Since late July 2011, the Company and CXT have been working with material scientists and prestressed concrete experts, who have been testing a representative sample of Grand Island concrete ties. While this testing is not complete, the Company has not identified any*

appreciable defects in workmanship. Additionally, a customer of the UPRR has claimed that a representative sample of ties manufactured by the Company's Grand Island facility have failed a test contained in its product specification. As a result of this specific allegation, the UPRR has informed the Company that they currently intend to remove approximately 115,000 ties from track, which are a subset of ties subject to the July 12, 2011 claim.

- *The Company is reviewing this claim and, while its review is not complete, the Company continues to believe that these ties do not have a material deviation from its contractual specifications. The Company expects that the testing required to address this product specification issue will be completed sometime during the latter part of the second quarter of 2012; however, the Company expects that it will continue to work collaboratively with the UPRR to address their overall product claim for some time to come.*
- *On January 11, 2012, CXT received a subpoena from the United States Department of Transportation Inspector General ("IG") requesting records related to its manufacture of concrete railroad ties in Grand Island, Nebraska. The Company believes that this subpoena relates to the same set of circumstances giving rise to the UPRR product claim. CXT and the Company intend to cooperate fully with the IG. The Company cannot predict what impact, if any, this investigation will have on the UPRR's product claim. Based on the non-specific nature of the UPRR's assertion and the Company's current inability to verify the claims, the Company is unable to determine a range of reasonably possible outcomes regarding this potential exposure matter. As a result,*

no accruals have been made as a result of this claim, as the impact, if any, cannot be reasonably estimated at this time. No assurances can be given regarding the ultimate outcome of this matter. The ultimate resolution of this matter could have a material, adverse impact on the Company's financial statements, results of operations, liquidity and capital resources.

According to their warranty they owe 1.5 times the amount in question, which is 1.6 million.

- 1.6 millionX1.5=2.4 million in potential ties they would have to pay for.

Current price that I found for concrete ties is $42 a piece.

Let us assume for the sake of being cautious that they have to replace the entire 2.4 million ties.

- 2.4 million X $42=$100,800,000 in potential cost.

Even if it is only one half or one-quarter of the 2.4 million than it would be:

- 1.2 million X$42=$50.4 million.
- 0.8 million X$42=$33.6 million.
- If it is only the 115,000 ties that need replacing: 115,000X1.5=172,500 ties.
- 172,500X$42=$7.245 million.

L.B. Foster currently has around $68 million in cash on hand. They have $124 million in a revolving credit line that they could use if needed. So they should be covered even in the absolute worst case scenario.

However, if it is the full $100.8 million amount, that is more than one-third of their current market cap, and almost one half of their enterprise value. Shocking amounts to me for a company of its size.

L.B. Foster has currently only made a reserve of $6.8 million to cover defective ties in this potential situation, which will not even fully cover the absolute minimum case.

As of the most recent 10Q, after analyzing some of the so called defective concrete ties, L.B. Foster has not found any defects in their concrete ties, which is of course very good news.

At worst this could be devastating to L.B. Foster going forward. If they have to draw down the credit facility they would not be able to fund future growth, make acquisitions, and probably have to stop paying the dividend that they just started. This could also lead to mistrust, loss of faith, and loss of confidence in L.B. Foster.

At best this could turn out to be a minor blip on the radar screen and amount to only a few million dollars worth of ties having to be repaid under the warranty.

There is currently too much uncertainty with the potential warranty claim for me to be a buyer in L.B. Foster at this time. In the meantime, I will continue to research L.B. Foster, and I will reassess after there is some conclusion to the warranty claim to determine if I will be a buyer at that time or not.

I did not talk about L.B. Foster's competitors because I cannot to a good degree. Two of their competitors are private companies who do not release financial information.

Alstom, the other company listed as a competitor to L.B. Foster, is not really a true competitor as they conduct most of their business in the thermal power area. They also do most of their business outside of the US, where L.B. Foster does almost all of their business.

So all I can really say about L.B. Foster and their competition is what L.B. Foster says in their SEC filings: That they are in highly competitive businesses, have to compete on pricing, and have to place highly competitive bids for jobs.

Analysis Explanation

I made a major misjudgment when evaluating L.B. Foster and have missed out on a near double to this point. As I stated above I am an extremely conservative investor but in this case was overly conservative and fixated on an unrealistic worst case scenario. When evaluating L.B. Foster's potential liability claim I paid too much attention to the absolute worst case scenario and thinking that they would have to repay $100 million worth of concrete ties.

If evaluating the same situation over again I would have realized that this was an impossible scenario as that amount of ties was not even in question and that only 115,000 of the concrete ties were in question of being defective. If all of those 115K concrete ties would have been defective they would have had to replace 1.5X that amount, or 172,500 ties. Current price of concrete ties when writing the original article was around $42 a piece so even in the worst case scenario they would have had to only pay $7.245 million. That is a far cry from the $100 million "worst case scenario" I was fixated on at that time. At the time of this writing, because of the extreme conservatism and misjudgment I have missed out on owning this company that has nearly doubled.

This is also a major reason that if you are to become a serious investor you need to read company filings because I would have never even known about the liability claim if I had not read its annual and quarterly reports and only relied on what was stated on financial websites and the company website. You would be surprised how often there are things like this in a company's financial reports that could cause some trouble and again recommend reading at absolute minimum the company's most recent annual, quarterly, and proxy reports and preferably 5+ years of financial information. I know this sounds like a lot, and it can be if you are evaluating bigger companies, but it is worth it and will end up keeping you from losing money by spotting potential problem areas so you can factor those issues into your investment thesis.

Having a margin of safety when you buy into a company is of utmost importance when evaluating a company for a potential investment as a value investor.

Companies not being undervalued enough, or overvalued as is the case with most companies as of the time of this writing, is very important to know for a few reasons: 1) If you buy a good company at a fair value, or even better at a substantial discount to your estimate of its intrinsic value, you have a lot better chance of making money over time. 2) If you make a mistake in your valuations and analysis but are very conservative in your estimates and buy substantially below your estimate of intrinsic value then you still will have a chance to make money off of the transaction or at least limit your losses. 3) If you buy into companies that are overvalued you will have a lot harder time making money over time and could stand to lose a lot of money if you make mistakes in your analysis.

EBIT and Net Cash Valuation Explanation

This is a valuation learned from John Chew's csinvesting.org and the videos he has posted from Bruce Greenwald's valuation class he teaches at Columbia University. I cannot recommend csinvesting.org highly enough as that is one of the sites that I have learned the most from and start reading the blog from the beginning and take notes.

If you learn from just this one site, along with the book you are currently reading, my blog, and a couple other sites that will mentioned throughout this book you will improve your investing knowledge immensely. I also guarantee that you will know more than most people who invest money, including most MBA's and professionals, about how to value and analyze a company for a potential investment as well.

The EBIT and net cash valuation is my favorite valuation technique and the one I use the most to this day. Use a company's trailing twelve month (TTM) EBIT, or operating profit, numbers to get the truest picture of how the company's operations should be valued at that particular moment. To calculate the TTM EBIT for a company you need the company's most recent annual report and most recent quarterly report where you calculate the TTM EBIT from the trailing twelve months.

If the company has recently come out with its annual report than you can just use that. You can adjust the TTM EBIT number further if the need arises by subtracting onetime, non recurring expenses which will generally be talked about in the company's footnotes. If you do subtract these items make sure that they are actually not recurring every year or relatively often as some companies say that they have one time or non recurring expenses but they end up happening every year or every few years like clockwork which obviously means that they are normal expenses which should be included in the TTM EBIT calculation. I use a range of between 5X and 14X + cash and cash equivalents as estimates of intrinsic value.

Most people would say that 5X EBIT estimate is too low in most cases but I use that to see what a company should be valued at using a very conservative multiple. Generally 8X EBIT+cash and cash equivalents is my base estimate of value and typically only use the 11 and 14 times EBIT numbers as either the high estimate of value. I will also use the 11 and 14 times EBIT estimates of value if the company has long-term sustainable competitive advantages, or a moat, which will be talked about later.

Most people use the net cash calculation to see how "healthy" the particular company's short term balance sheet is. I use the net cash part of this valuation just as one basis for how healthy I think a company's balance sheet is and do not put too much stock into the net cash valuation alone unless the number is either hugely negative or positive in relation to the company's share price. We will talk more in-depth later on how to see if a company has a healthy balance sheet but this is just one small early part of the puzzle in that regard.

Another reason I like this valuation beside its general ease of use is that this valuation can be combined with other valuation techniques which is something that will be shown later.

Something that I use more now than then is the EV/EBIT ratio, or enterprise value to operating profit ratio. This is one kind of what are called relative valuations where you compare certain ratios like this one, and others that will be shown later, to other companies to see which company is valued relatively the lowest. This is a metric I use all the time now and will explain it in-depth more later but generally I like to see a company's EV/EBIT ratio under 8 when thinking about buying into that company. The reason this ratio should be under 8 is because of an interview on a website I found where Warren Buffett said that if you buy good companies at EV/EBIT ratios of 8 and under, generally and over the long-term you will end up doing very well investing. So far my experience has confirmed Mr. Buffett's thoughts on this matter.

Chapter 6: Altria (MO) August 2012. Free Cash Flow, Revenue and EBIT Valuations. Debt, Pensions, Interest Rates, Litigation, Competitive Advantages, Off Balance Sheet Commitments, Book, and Site Recommendations.

"Spend each day trying to be a little wiser than you were when you woke up." Charlie Munger

When I first started reading about Altria, (MO) its dividend is what initially got me very intrigued. Altria was the first company that I bought where I actually read an annual report so it was my starting point for the research I am doing now. However, I was not doing any type of valuation or near the amount of research I am doing now so I got a bit lucky that my position is now up around 30%. I started doing this write-up and research of Altria mainly to see how far I had come since I originally bought earlier in 2011.

However, now that I have just read its most recent 10K and 10Q I have found many things that bother me about the company.

First I will give the reasons why I originally bought more than a year ago:

- Big dividend in a low yield environment, the dividend has been growing as well.
- Huge competitive advantages that I noticed even then: Addicted customers who were willing to keep paying higher and higher prices. A government sponsored mini-monopoly since there aren't likely to be any new entrants due to litigation and taxes. Massive brand recognition and market share.
- They were producing about $3 billion in FCF per year, which I thought was enough to cover the dividend.

Risks I saw then:

- Massive debt load over $12 billion.
- Litigation expenses.

Those were literally the only two concerns I had, and the only major concern of the two was the debt. Altria seems to win a lot of its lawsuits or if they do lose, they end up having the amount to be paid out cut substantially, so that did not worry me too much.

The above are literally the **only** things I looked at before deciding to buy MO last year. This is not very in-depth thinking and definitely not enough to get me even close to a buy or sell decision today.

Analysis now

Altria comprises Philip Morris USA, U.S. Smokeless Tobacco Company, John Middleton, Ste. Michelle Wine Estates, and Philip Morris Capital Corporation. It also owns a 27.1% interest in SABMiller, the world's second-largest brewer. Through its tobacco subsidiaries, Altria holds the leading position in cigarettes and smokeless tobacco in the United States and the number-two spot in cigars. The company's Marlboro brand is the leading cigarette brand in the U.S.

Having sold its international segments and the bulk of its nontobacco assets, Altria now operates primarily in the challenging U.S. tobacco industry. U.S. cigarette volume is in secular decline, and the Food and Drug Administration, having assumed regulatory control, has been quick to assert its authority. The threats of regulation and taxation have now overtaken litigation as the most significant risks to an investment in tobacco, in our view. Despite these headwinds, tobacco manufacturing is still a lucrative business, and we think Altria is poised to generate steady medium-term earnings growth. The addictive nature of cigarettes and Altria's dominance of the U.S. market is the key reasons behind our wide economic moat rating.

The two descriptions above are taken from Morningstar.com.

Valuations:

Valuations were done using 2011 10K and second quarter 2012 10Q. All numbers are in millions of US dollars, except per share information, unless otherwise noted. Valuations were done on July 27th 2012.

Net cash and EBIT valuation:

Altria has cash and cash equivalents of 1,528.

Its number of shares outstanding is 2,027.

Altria has total current liabilities of 6,081.

Cash and cash equivalents-total current liabilities=1528-6081=-4553.

- -4553/2027=-$2.25 of net cash per share.

Altria has a trailing twelve month EBIT of 3519+6068-1295-1539=6753.

5X, 8X, 11X, and 14X EBIT+cash and cash equivalents=

- 5X6753=33765+1528=35293/2027=$17.41 per share
- 8X6753=54024+1528=55552/2027=$27.41 per share
- 11X6753=74283+1528=75811/2027=$37.40 per share
- 14X6753=94542+1528=96070/2027=$47.40 per share

Current price is $35.63 per share.

Market cap is 72.44 billion.

Enterprise value is 84.44 billion.

- EV/EBIT=12.50

My average unit cost including dividends is currently $27.10 per share for the MO shares I currently own.

Only the 14X EBIT valuation would get me a reasonable margin of safety if I were to buy now. If I were to buy MO shares now I would be using either the 11X or 14X EBIT valuations as my base case.

A couple things of note: Altria has a negative net cash number which I generally do not like.
Altria's EV/EBIT is higher than the companies I usually evaluate, which is another sign that it might be fairly or overvalued currently.

Revenue and EBIT valuation:

Using trailing twelve month numbers:

Revenue: 16,670

Multiplied By:

Average 4 year EBIT percentage: 34.13%

Equals:

Estimated EBIT of: 5,689.47

Multiplied by:

Assumed fair value multiple of EBIT: 10X

Equals:

Estimated fair value Enterprise value of MO: 56,894.7

Plus:

Cash and Cash equivalents: 1,528

Minus:

Total Debt: 13,089

Equals:

Estimated fair value of common equity: 45,333.7

Divided by:

Number of shares: 2,027

Equals:

$22.36 per share.

Low estimate

My high estimate of value, which I would use as my base estimate of value in this case, was a 15X estimated EBIT multiple which came out to $36.40 per share, about evenly valued.

Free cash flow valuation:

Again, using trailing twelve month numbers.

Operating cash flow: 3,388

Minus:

Capital expenditures: 108

Equals:

Free cash flow (FCF): 3,280

Divided by:

Industry median FCF yield: 6%

Equals:

Industry FCF yield implied fair value: 54,666.67 ($26.97 per share.)

Multiplied by:

Assumed required FCF yield as a percentage of industry FCF yield: 95%

Equals:

Estimated fair value of common equity of MO: 51,933.34

Divided by:

Number of shares: 2,027

Equals:

$25.62 per share.

Low estimate

My high estimate, where I changed the assumed yield from 95% to 125% came out to $33.71 per share.

I would estimate its intrinsic value to be the 11X EBIT multiple from the net cash and EBIT valuation, $37.40 per share.

Through these valuations I have found Altria to be either overvalued or about fairly valued at current prices. Looks like I got a bit lucky when I was doing no valuations, or the amount of research I am doing now, when I bought MO around $27 per share.

I was mainly doing this exercise to see how far I have come since I originally bought MO; doing no valuations and minimal research. My intention when I started this was not to do a complete analysis, but I found a few things that gave me some pause while reading its SEC filings that I wanted to highlight.

Concerns:

- All the litigation, which I will not detail here since it takes up at least 50 pages of the 10K. If you would like further information please read Altria's annual reports.
- Altria has been issuing debt and drawing on its short-term credit line to in part sustain its stock repurchasing and dividend.
- Debt of around $13 billion, around $11 billion of which came from its acquisition of US Tobacco in 2009. Altria almost immediately charged about $5 billion of the transaction price to goodwill, meaning that that they paid almost double the price of the assets. Quoting from the 10K "The excess of the purchase price paid by Altria Group, Inc. over the fair value of identifiable net assets acquired in the acquisition of UST primarily reflects the value of adding USSTC and its subsidiaries to Altria Group, Inc.'s family of tobacco operating companies (PM USA and Middleton), with leading brands in cigarettes, smokeless products and machine-made large cigars,

and anticipated annual synergies of approximately $300 million resulting primarily from reduced selling, general and administrative, and corporate expenses. None of the goodwill or other intangible assets will be deductible for tax purposes." To me paying almost double the price of the assets for supposed synergies does not make much sense and will also make it take longer for Altria to earn back its investment.
- Altria has projected pension and health obligations of around $6.5 billion. The projected amount has been rising by around $500 million a year for the last few years as well.
- Altria has total off-balance sheet arrangements and aggregate contractual obligations of $33.7 billion, most of which are coming due after 2017, with around $4 billion a year needing to be paid over the next few years. The total obligations include: Debt, Interest on borrowings, Operating leases, Purchase obligations, and other long-term liabilities.
- Altria's fair value of total debt as of the most recent 10K is $17.7 billion. A 1% point increase in market interest rates would decrease the fair value of Altria Group, Inc's total debt by approximately $1.1 billion. A 1% point decrease in market interest rates would increase the fair value of Altria Group Inc's total debt by approximately $1.2 billion. This risk is taken directly from its

10K on page 95 of the final section of the 10K. Since interest rates cannot go any lower, and will not stay low forever, rising rates are going to crush the debt of Altria unless it can refinance portions of the debt, which could also make it harder for them to issue debt in the future.
- The above are not even including the dropping rate of smoking in the US, and state and federal governments around the country regulating the tobacco industry so strictly that it has turned into a prohibition like industry.
- People have been piling into the stock recently for the high yield, which could be turning into a mini bubble around the stock and other high yield companies.
- Will not grow outside of the US. That was the whole reason for the spin-off of Philip Morris (PM) so that Altria would have the US market, and PM would have the international markets.
- Insiders only own 0.08% of company stock.
- Since Altria does have a high debt load, it could preclude them from acquiring companies until it pays down some of the debt.

Pros:

- Altria has ownership of one of the most recognized brands in the world, Marlboro.

- Altria has 50% market share of the cigarette market in the US.
- Altria has 55% market share in the smokeless products in the US.
- Altria also has 30% market share in the cigar market in the US.
- Altria own a 27% interest in SABMiller, valued currently at about $19 billion. Altria could sell this asset if they needed to pay down debt.
- Altria creates about $3 billion a year in FCF.
- Its margins are gigantic: Gross margin at 54%, EBIT margin at 37%, ROIC at 19%, and FCF/Sales margin at 20%.
- Addicted customers.
- Because governments regulate the tobacco industry a lot, Altria will not have to deal with any new entrants any time soon.
- Competitive advantages: Economies of scale, quasi government sanctioned monopoly.

How I think they could improve further:

Paying down the substantial debt would be a great step in the right direction. In my opinion Altria should become a conglomerate, kind of a Berkshire Hathaway sin stock conglomerate. Altria already owns a wine company subsidiary, and it owns part of one of the biggest beer producers in the world, and I think that MO could get further into that arena if they wanted to.

Altria could produce and sell marijuana when and if that ever becomes legalized since it would have the distribution lines already available. Altria could also buy a company like Star Scientific (CIGX). Here is Morningstar's description of them, Star Scientific, along with its subsidiary, Star Tobacco, is a technology-oriented tobacco company seeking to develop, license, and implement technology to reduce the carcinogenic toxins in tobacco and tobacco smoke.

I remember reading a while ago that there was a rumor that either Altria or Philip Morris could buy CIGX to develop next generation cigarettes that did not have the carcinogens in them, thus alleviating the main concern with smoking. I have not read any more rumors of that in a long time though.

One thing that is for certain, although smoking will never go away no matter how much governments regulate and tax the industry, Altria in my opinion, will eventually have to branch out at least a little bit due to declining rates of smoking in the US.

Conclusion:

Altria is one of the most dominant companies in the world. It has a virtual monopoly in the United States in the cigarette and smokeless product segments, with at least 50% market share in both of those two industry segments. The company has incredible competitive advantages that enable it to continue to have huge margins even with all the litigation, taxes, and regulation.

The company is not perfect as it has a myriad of issues that I outlined above. If you were to buy Altria at the current prices, it appears that you would have no margin of safety and I would not recommend buying at this time.

However, I think the positives outweigh the negatives at the $27 price that I bought at, and I plan to hold onto my shares of Altria for hopefully decades, and hope to have my money compound well into the future, if Altria can get its debt and pension obligations under control that should be no problem.

Analysis Explanation

This is my most viewed and commented on article on Seeking Alpha and for further discussion and an opportunity for further learning highly recommend going to my author profile on Seeking Alpha and the link is listed in chapter 3. The comments on this article are amazing and you will learn a lot from what some of the commenter's said.

This is also going to be one of the biggest and potentially most important chapters in this book because of the amount of information that is in it. You will be introduced to a slew of new valuation techniques, talk about pensions and debt and how to analyze them and factor them into your analysis. We will also talk about litigation, government intervention, and introduce a bunch of new terms. If you are feeling overwhelmed by this chapter read through it entirely once, look up some of the terms, try some of the valuation techniques for yourself, and go to this article on Seeking Alpha, and then come back and reread the chapter as it is a very important one.

Before doing the analysis on Altria I stopped evaluating companies and reading their annual reports for a while so I could concentrate on learning new things to incorporate into the evaluations.

As I talked about in the article, I owned Altria for a while and it was actually one of the first companies that I bought stock into when actually reading an annual report before buying into them. I did not write an article on them until later and as talked about at the beginning of the chapter my original thought process was very limited in comparison to the actual analysis wrote down later. I would like to illustrate the value of writing your ideas and analysis down. Writing your ideas down, even if you do not share them with anyone else on a blog or elsewhere on the web, is extremely important.

The original unwritten thought process here was very limited and not substantial enough to make a proper investment decision. Writing your ideas down enables you to see your thoughts on the screen or paper and will help you to see if you are missing anything in your analysis. As you can see when comparing the before and after, I missed a lot in the original investment thesis with Altria and was lucky to get out making money. You can get some very objective and good feedback if you do start a blog or post your analysis on other sites like Seeking Alpha or GuruFocus also and that is something I cannot recommend highly enough. Yes a lot of the updated Altria analysis was after learning a lot of new techniques and things to look for, but I still missed a lot of specific things, especially in relation to debt and pension analysis since I was new to learning about those then. I would not have thought to write about those or realized that the analysis of them was wrong until writing my thoughts down.

The main points of interest in the analysis of Altria were that they had massive long-term competitive advantages brought on by the addiction of its products and through government litigation and intervention in its industry, it's fantastic margins, the free cash flow it creates, the big dividend it pays, along with some of the other things talked about in the article.

- Long Term Sustainable Competitive Advantages or Moats: Competitive advantages are things to look for and be cherished by investors as they can mean that the company earns high returns on its invested capital as Altria does. Return on invested capital, or ROIC, is in my opinion the most important profitability metric and companies that can earn ROICs of 10% and above for long periods of time are generally fantastic companies to own, especially if they are undervalued or fairly valued. A high ROIC that is sustained over many years may also mean that the company has a long-term competitive advantage. The two books I have read that are best at explaining competitive advantages and the power they can create for the companies that have them are Competition Demystified and Repeatability, both of which are highly recommend, and they do a better job of explaining competitive advantages than I ever could. Also if you are interested in learning more about competitive advantages search my blog or

Google Warren Buffett, Charlie Munger, moats, and/or competitive advantages.

Revenue and EBIT Valuation Explanation

This valuation is another one that I use quite often as it can be used in most situations. Generally this valuation is used to get an idea of how a company should be valued based on its recent historical EBIT margin. I generally use a three or five-year EBIT margin average in the calculation. The reason this is useful, especially with the recent recession, is so you can see how a company operated during the recession compared to how they are now operating. Being an extremely conservative investor I like to see how a company handled the proverbial worst case scenario and factor that into the valuations and analysis going forward. I use the companies trailing twelve month revenue and EBIT in the valuations. Since you are using a historical EBIT average over several years I do not adjust that number in this valuation. I multiply EBIT using the same range used in the earlier EBIT and net cash valuation (5-14X) in this one as well, generally only using the 11 and 14X EBIT ranges with companies who have long-term sustainable competitive advantages or as my high estimates of value.

Free cash flow Valuation Explanation

This valuation is used with companies that create a lot of or consistent free cash flow (FCF). I do not use this valuation that much anymore now that I am concentrating on micro and nano-caps (smaller companies that generally have market caps under $100 million and generally do not create consistent positive FCF) but if you are going to be concentrating on bigger companies or companies that create consistent FCF this is a very good valuation to use.

I always use TTM numbers for operating cash flow, capital expenditures, and free cash flow. As with the adjusting of EBIT, these numbers can also be adjusted to exclude things like one time and non recurring payments. If a company is creating consistent FCF and has solid plans to lower cap ex in the very near future, and you trust that management will do that, you can subtract that estimated number from cap ex which will give you a higher estimate of FCF.

- To find FCF yield you take FCF per share and divide it by current market price per share.

After doing this for each company you add those numbers together and then divide that by the number of companies you calculated for to find the estimated industry FCF yield. The assumed required FCF yield as a percentage of industry FCF yield is an estimate of the percentage that the company is earning in comparison to its industry.

Assuming a lower percentage will yield a lower intrinsic value estimate, and a higher percentage will yield a higher intrinsic value estimate. As with the other valuations I like to use a range of estimates. Generally the low estimate is between 50 and 60% of the industry percentage, base estimate is in the 75% range, and high range is usually 90% to 125% depending on the company. For companies who are not as stable or that do not create consistent positive FCF I use the lower estimates, and if the company is like Altria where it dominates its industry, creates consistent positive FCF, and has competitive advantages I use the higher estimates.

Both of these valuation techniques were learned from the Manual of Ideas free newsletter that they gave out a while ago where the only "cost" was Tweeting out that you downloaded the newsletter for free to your followers. You can find the link to this newsletter by searching for Manual of Ideas on my blog. Some of the other valuation techniques that have been or will be talked about in this book came from that one free download as well. Excellent return on your investment and as you will see throughout this book, and have shown on my blog, you can find many free resources like this online that are the equivalent of going to a college class on valuation.

There were also some other valuation techniques for specific industries such as how to value oil and gas companies, and how to value mining companies, that I will not talk about in this book. I do not research those companies because I do not understand how to evaluate them properly but if you are interested in learning how to value those kinds of companies I recommend the Manual of Ideas free download that is mentioned above.

Pensions

Pensions and how to evaluate how they affect the company you are researching is one of the more important things you can learn to help when evaluating a company. Although pensions on a large-scale aren't used as much as they used to be, they can still greatly affect a company's future and current profitability. Using Altria as an example: Altria has projected pension and health obligations of around $6.5 billion. The projected amount has risen by around $500 million a year for the last few years as well. Altria at that time had 2.027 billion shares meaning that it had $3.21 per share in pension obligations and those total pension obligations had risen by around $500 million a year on average over the past several years, or adding another 25 cents per share to the total pension obligations per share every year.

To illustrate how much money this is we are going to use an extreme example. Let us say that Altria decided to pay down all of those pensions, that would potentially add $3.21 per share a year to earnings, and earnings would be further improved by another 25 cents per year due to pension costs not rising every year for a total gain to earnings in its first year after paying down all of those obligations of $3.46 per share.

If I remember right Altria was selling for a PE around 15 at that time meaning it had earnings of around $1.80 per share. If Altria were able to get rid of all of its pensions and then letting that money move its way over to earnings it would almost triple current earnings. If Altria were still to sell for a PE of around 15 after that happened, with earnings of $5.26 per share, Altria stock would be worth $78.90 per share instead of the $27 when originally bought.

Yes the above is in extreme example because pension obligations are generally only paid out years, and possibly decades in advance, but this is the kind of strain pension obligations can put on how a company is operating in the present as they still have to count these kinds of things on the company's current balance sheet and account for these kinds of future expenses now, which affect profitability and cash flow in the present.

Competitive Advantages

We will continue to talk about competitive advantages or moats as they are also called, in many of the rest of the chapters in this book so I will not elaborate too much on it now as we will continue to see throughout the rest of this book why they are so important. For now though these are some of the most desirable things to find in a company and can be incredibly valuable over years and decades. These are generally things like a dominant position in a particular market or industry, dominant market share, patents that will keep competitors away, government regulations that will keep competitors away, network effects like Amazon or Facebook where because a lot of people use those sites, more people will continue to use those sites, etc.

Again I highly recommend reading the following books and searching for the following things on my blog, CSInvesting, or Google on this topic: Competition Demystified, Repeatability, Buffett and/or Munger on Competitive advantages, competitive advantage case studies on Amazon, Wal-Mart, Altria/Philip Morris, Coca-Cola, and WD-40. Finding a company with a competitive advantage is not really that hard, finding a company that has a competitive advantage that is sustainable over years and decades is.

If you can find a company with a long-term sustainable competitive advantage that is undervalued, you will do very well investing over time. Later there will be some chapters where I will illustrate companies that I have found that do not have a moat and how that affects them and their competition and you will also see a couple companies that do have at least a small competitive advantage and how that favorably affects them.

Litigation/Government Regulations

Obviously litigation is generally not a good thing for a company to be involved in for decades at a time as it can not only cost a lot of money if you are found guilty, it also takes a lot of time, and can distract companies away from concentrating their focus on how to grow and make the company more profitable. However, Altria generally seems to come out pretty well in the many cases that have come against it and is generally either found not guilty. If it is found guilty the amount that is supposed to be paid out is generally only a fraction of the originally sought amount.

Being in the smoking and smokeless tobacco industry Altria on a yearly basis faces many charges that it has to refute and it has generally seemed to have little effect on the company and it being the dominant company in those markets in the United States.

Including the litigation Altria and its other tobacco competitors in the US (the same happens abroad as well as I learned from owning Philip Morris for a while) the tobacco companies face very onerous state and federal government regulations on what it can and cannot do. The government entities have also enacted very heavy taxes on tobacco related products which along with the very stringent regulations and litigation has helped to eat into the tobacco companies profitability.

However, Altria has remained very profitable over the years even with these things going against them and partly because of them in my opinion. Due to all the litigation, taxes, and regulations tobacco companies face it is not very likely that a big new competitor will enter the field to shake things up by cutting prices. This has helped sustain and strengthen Altria's competitive advantages as it has remained the dominant force in the US market for years. These kinds of competitive advantages brought on by excessive government regulation, taxes, and litigation make it highly undesirable and most likely impossible for smaller more creative companies to enter the market to innovate and possibly change the industry. So unless Altria does something incredibly stupid or smoking becomes banned outright, (Which would be an absolute disaster as we saw with Prohibition) or a new product comes around that completely disrupts the entire industry then Altria should stay the dominant force in the industry for years to come.

This kind of long-term sustainable competitive advantage brought on by government intervention can make the companies at the top very profitable for long periods of time and if it can be found in an undervalued company, could make you a lot of money.

Interest Rates/Debt

Interest rates are very important when considering an equity investment as well as a bond investment. Prominent investors say that you should aim/expect to return at minimum on your equity investments two or three times the current 10 year Treasury yield. For example with a 10 year Treasury yield at 5%, you should aim to return on your equity investment at least 10 to 15% over time. This does not sound like much, but over time if you can earn 10 to 15% on your money you will be doing very well. Warren Buffett has earned around a 20% return on his money every year for over 40 years and look how well he is doing.

Interest rates affect many things in an equity investment but the main thing we are going to talk about here is a company's debt. At the time I did the write up on Altria it had debt and total obligations of $33.7 billion, $17 billion of which was considered interest bearing. I now almost always use and combine the debt and total obligations in my calculations as I think that shows a truer picture of how the company is operating and is something that we will talk more about and how to capitalize leases and such later. For this example though we will be using the $17 billion and most of the debt came due after 2017. Directly from Altria's most recent annual report at that time: **A 1% point increase in market interest rates would decrease the fair value of Altria Group, Inc's total debt by about $1.1 billion. A 1% point decrease in market interest rates would increase the fair value of Altria Group Inc's total debt by about $1.2 billion.**

Debt is inverted as an increase in interest rates decreases value of the bonds and a decrease in interest rates increases the value of the bonds. Because interest rates are being manipulated lower right now, this means that once rates start to go up every 1% point increase in interest rates will lead to Altria's bonds losing $1.2 billion in value. Not good eh? This does not even consider that as its debt load rises that when interest rates rise that if it has to continue to issue debt that it will be at higher interest rates, meaning higher and higher interest payments, and less money going towards the company's bottom line if they do not change something.

Being an extremely conservative investor I generally hate debt, especially large sums of it like Altria has, and try to steer clear of companies with a lot of it. What bothered me even more after I actually fully analyzed Altria though was not the debt itself, it was that Altria was issuing debt in recent years to sustain its share buybacks and ever-growing dividend as the free cash flow that it is creating was not enough to continue both the buybacks and the dividend by itself.

Not only had Altria taken on around $12 billion in debt with its US Tobacco acquisition, it has continued to issue debt, becoming more financially insecure just to sustain its dividend and buybacks. This is insane to me and conservative value investing habits. The amounts of money are staggering and scare me now as an investor which is just one of the reasons I have now sold all of my stock in Altria. The other main reason was because at this point I was gaining a lot of confidence in what I was doing and decided to start looking for smaller companies to buy into that I believe have a far greater upside than a giant company like Altria does.

Chapter 7: Jack in the Box (JACK) October 2012. Price To Book and Tangible Book Valuation. Why You Must Do Your Own Research, Hype, Catalysts, Comparison To Competition, and Site Recommendation.

"It's easy to fall into the trap of believing all the hype that's written about you....Who knows? In a couple of years, you might find me in the loony bin!" Leonardo DiCaprio

Recently I have seen a bit about Jack in the Box (JACK) and its long-term potential through a possible spin-off down the road of its subsidiary Qdoba, the entire company being bought out by one of the bigger fast food chains, or though its margin growth now that it has about 72% of its Jack in the Box fast food restaurants being owned by franchisees. Franchise royalty margins I have seen estimated as high as 80%.

After seeing all the above and how undervalued everyone seems to think JACK now is, I decided to research the company myself. Most of what I have read about JACK from other people is that it is undervalued because of the "Future potential" of the company with what I talked about in the first paragraph given as reasons; a lot of ifs in every pro JACK article I have read thus far. As you know I do not operate on ifs and future potential. With the rest of this article I will be showing you why I think JACK is overvalued and give you reasons why I will not be investing in it at this time.

Jack In the Box Overview

JACK owns and operates a total of 2,247 Jack in the Box fast food restaurants, about 72% of which are owned by franchisees. Jack in the Box is one of the largest hamburger chains in the US with operations in 19 states, with the vast majority of its operations in California and Texas. JACK also owns Qdoba and has 614 total restaurants, about half of which are owned by franchisees. Qdoba is a fast food Mexican restaurant with operations in 44 states. For further information on JACK please visit its website.

Jack in the Box has recently finished up reimaging some of its restaurants by changing the logo, updating the menu, and making its restaurants look more modern. The recent reimaging of Jack in the Box restaurants has led to higher capital expenditures and sometimes lower revenues over recent years. Now that the bulk of the reimaging is done, Jack in the Box is hoping to become even more profitable.

In recent years Jack in the Box has under gone the process of selling some of its restaurants to franchisees so it can get into the higher margin area of collecting royalty and franchise fees. Jack in the Box now has around 72% of its restaurants owned by franchisees with plans to eventually have 80% of its restaurants owned by franchisees.

Qdoba has gone through a rapid growth phase since being acquired by JACK in 2003 and JACK management states that it believes there is future potential of between 1,800 and 2,000 Qdoba restaurants in the United States.

As of the most recent 10Q, JACK gets 56.9% of its revenue from sales at its restaurants, 27.7% from distribution sales, and 15.5% from franchise and royalties. Total company costs are 83.5% of total revenues which come from food and packaging 32.3%, payroll and employee benefits 28.7%, and occupancy and other 22.5%.

Valuations

All numbers are in millions of US dollars, except per share information, unless otherwise noted. The following valuations were done using its 2011 10K and 3Q 2012 10Q.

I did my other normal valuations as well but from now on plan to only post the ones that I think are most relevant.

Low Estimate of Value:

Assets:	Book Value:	Reproduction Value:
Current Assets		
Cash & Cash Equivalents	10.8	10.8
Accounts Receivable & Other Receivables (Net)	84.9	72.2
Inventories	37	18.5
Prepaid Expenses	32.2	16
Deferred Income Tax - Deferred Tax Liability	39	19.5

Assets Held For Sale & Leaseback	62.4	31
Other Current Assets	1	0
Total Current Assets	267.3	168
PP&E Net	825.5	495.3
Goodwill	140.5	84.3
Other Assets Net	241	120
Total Assets	1474	867.6

Number of shares are 45

Reproduction value:

- Without goodwill: 783.3/45=$17.40 per share.

Base Estimate of Value:

Cash and cash equivalents are 10.8

Short term investments are 0

Total current liabilities are 266

Number of shares are 45

Cash and cash equivalents + short-term investments - total current liabilities=

- 10.8+0-266=-255.2/45=-$5.67 in net cash per share.

Jack in the Box has a trailing twelve month EBIT of 120.

5X, 8X, 11X, and 14X EBIT + cash and cash equivalents + short-term investments:

- 5X120=600+10.8=610.8
- 8X120=960+10.8=970.8
- 11X120=1320+10.8=1330.8
- 14X120=1680+10.8=1690.8
- 5X=610.8/45=$13.57 per share.
- 8X=970.8/45=$21.57 per share.
- 11X=1330.8/45=$29.57 per share.
- 14X=1690.8/45=$37.57 per share.

From this valuation I would use the 8X EBIT and cash estimate of intrinsic value, $21.57 per share.

High Estimates Of Value:

	Numbers:
Revenue:	2165

Multiplied By:	
Average 5 year EBIT %:	7.50%
Equals:	
Estimated EBIT of:	162.4
Multiplied By:	
Assumed Fair Value Multiple of EBIT:	11X
Equals:	
Estimated Fair Enterprise Value of JACK:	1786.4
Plus:	
Cash, Cash Equivalents, and Short Term Investments:	10.8
Minus:	

Total Debt:	451
Equals:	
Estimated Fair Value of Common Equity:	1346.2
Divided By:	
Number of Shares:	45
Equals:	$29.92 per share.

Price To Book and Tangible Book Valuation:

	Numbers:
Book Value:	490.5
Minus:	
Intangibles:	140.5

Equals:	
Tangible Book Value:	350
Multiplied By:	
Industry P/B:	6.4
Equals:	
Industry Multiple Implied Fair Value:	2240
Multiplied By:	
Assumed Multiple as a Percentage of Industry Multiple:	75%
Equals:	
Estimated Fair Value of Common Equity:	1680
Divided By:	

Number of Shares:	50
Equals:	$33.60 per share.

I will explain my reasons for picking these valuations in the conclusions portion of this article, but by my estimates JACK Is currently either fairly valued or overvalued by almost every valuation technique I did, except for the valuations with very high multiples.

Margins and Debt In Comparison To Competitors

	Jack in the Box (JACK)	Sonic Corp (SONC)	McDonald's (MCD)	Yum Brands (YUM)	Chipotle Mexican Grill (CMG)	Avg
Gross Margin 5 Year Average	16.28%	34.30%	37.94%	26.20%	24.28%	27.80%
Gross Margin 10 Year Average	17.08%	43.38%	40.42%	35.59%	11.73%	29.04%
Op Margin 5 Year Average	7.46%	16.24%	27.42%	14.22%	12.76%	15.62%
Op Margin 10 Year Average	7.07%	18.05%	22.62%	13.50%	6.64%	13.57%
ROE 5 Year Average	20.16%	66.33%	30.26%	131.56%	18.55%	53.37%
ROE 10 Year Average	18.77%	43.71%	23.19%	105.85%	10.27%	40.36%
ROIC 5 Year Average	11.17%	3.38%	17.38%	24.97%	18.49%	15.08%
ROIC 10 Year Average	10.91%	8.97%	13.37%	23.54%	10.22%	13.40%
FCF/Sales 5 Year Average	-0.26%	6.48%	15.90%	7.70%	6.92%	7.35%
FCF/Sales 10 Year Average	0.80%	7.10%	12.86%	6.70%	2.26%	5.94%
Cash Conversion Cycle 5 Year Average	0.78	1.23	0.91	-36.35	-5.24	-7.92

Cash Conversion Cycle 10 Year Average	0.27	1.14	-1.22	-49.02	-5.21	-10.81
P/B Current	2.9	12.4	6.7	14.3	8.2	8.9
Insider Ownership Current	0.38%	6.12%	0.07%	0.50%	1.64%	1.74%
EV/EBIT Current	14.25	9.65	12.16	15.81	26.53	15.68
Debt Comparisons						
Total Debt as a % of Balance Sheet 5 year Average	30.78%	80.91%	35.28%	45.24%	0	38.44%
Total debt as a % of Balance Sheet 10 year Average	26.84%	50.77%	35.22%	40.72%	0.14%	30.74%
Current Assets to Current Liabilities	1.02	1.38	1.24	0.97	4.13	1.75
Total Debt to Equity	1.03	9.69	0.97	1.6	0	2.66
Total Debt to Total Assets	30.50%	71.20%	41%	37.21%	0	35.98%
Total Contractual Obligations and Commitment Including Debt	$2.6 Billion	$1 Billion	$27.20 Billion	$11.42 Billion	$2.20 Billion	$8.88 Billion
Total Obligations and Debt/EBIT	21.67	8.85	3.15	5.4	5.82	8.98

My thoughts on the above comparisons:

- McDonald's is by far the most profitable company of the five as it far out distances the competition in gross margin, operating or EBIT margin, FCF/sales, etc.
- Sonic and Yum Brands' ROE and ROIC are astounding but are inflated by both companies

high levels of debt in comparison to the other three companies.
- JACK's margins have generally declined in the last five years in comparison to the entire 10 year period. Most of the other company's margins during that time have improved.
- Chipotle's margins are pretty amazing, especially when you see that it does not have any debt so the numbers are not inflated like Sonic and Yum.
- On an EV/EBIT basis Chipotle looks to be very overvalued now with a ratio of 26.53.
- The insider ownership of all the companies is horrendous.
- The P/B of this industry is by far the highest I have seen since doing in-depth research.
- The EV/EBIT ratios are also much higher than the companies I have researched lately.
- The P/B and EV/EBIT ratios being much higher than what I have found lately leads me to believe that this entire industry is either fairly valued or overvalued now.
- The entire industry has some very high debt levels due to the costs of food, restaurant leases, etc. Debt levels have risen quite a bit recently as all the companies, with the exception of CMG and MCD, have taken on more debt in the past five years.
- MCD, YUM, and CMG's total obligations and debt/EBIT ratios look very sustainable into the future.
- JACK's total obligations and debt/EBIT ratio is dangerously high at 21.67. Especially of concern

is that the bulk of its obligations and debt are due before 2016.
- Sonics' debt levels also seem to be too high to me.
- Helping out SONC, MCD, YUM, and CMG is that most of the four company's debt and total obligations are coming due after 2016.

Let us now get back to JACK.

Pros

- JACK has bought back a lot of shares and has reduced its share count by 13 million since 2009, down to a total of 45 million as of the most recent quarter.
- JACK has decent margins that have been consistently positive over the past decade.
- Now that the reimaging of Jack in the Box is done cap ex should go down and profit margins should go up over time.
- Qdoba is a high growth asset that is also now more profitable than Jack in the box.
- JACK's debt ratios, excluding total obligations, all look very good compared to its competitors.
- Selling restaurants to franchisees will get JACK into the higher margin business of collecting royalty and franchise fees.
- Fortunately most of JACK's debt has low-interest rates.
- JACK owns the land underneath some of its restaurants which provides at least partial downside protection due to the possible sale of

the land if it was facing dire problems and was forced to sell some of its assets.

Cons

- JACK's debt ratios above are very misleading as they do not include contractual obligations and commitments.
- JACK's total obligations and debt in comparison to its profitability levels are way too high in my opinion with a total obligations/EBIT ratio of 21.67. This is by far the highest of the group and dangerously high in my opinion.
- Most of its debt and obligations are due within the next 5 years further exacerbating the debt situation in my eyes.
- Margins have been declining at JACK over the past five years, in part due to the reimagining of its Jack in the Box restaurants.
- JACK's margins while decent and relatively steady over the past few years, are also generally quite a bit lower than its competitors.
- JACK's FCF/sales margin is negative over the past five years while the industry average is 7.35% over that time.
- JACK is overvalued by almost every one of my estimates of intrinsic value.
- The entire fast food industry appears to be either fairly valued or overvalued at this time.
- About 85% of its revenues go towards paying costs, greatly affecting margins.
- JACK will continue to put a lot of its resources towards opening and running restaurants and

food costs. Some of the cost of new restaurants is paid by the developer however.
- A 1% point increase in short-term interest rates would result in an estimated increase of $3.6 million in annual interest expense. Interest rates can only go higher from where they are at now.
- Has a low amount of cash on hand.
- Managements pay seems too high to me.
- How JACK management structures the pay, bonuses, and awarding of options and restricted stock is very convoluted. The most recent proxy is longer than the most recent annual report, most of which is spent trying to explain how management is awarded some of its compensation.
- Horribly low insider ownership.
- I do not see any kind of moat or competitive advantages within JACK.

Potential Catalysts

- Margins should rise now that the store reimaging of Jack in the Box restaurants are done, which could eventually lead to a higher estimate of value.
- The total obligations and debt situation could be a negative catalyst if JACK should have any problems.
- As of the most recent proxy, Fidelity Management & Research Company owns 14.9% of JACK. If FMR decides to liquidate a portion or all of its position in JACK there could be a big sell off in the stock.

- If JACK management decides to sell or spin-off Qdoba it would send the stock price higher.
- JACK could be bought out by a bigger fast food chain.

Conclusion

The reason I chose the above estimates of intrinsic value, that I am sure the JACK bulls will say are too low, are because of the problems I found with JACK as it now stands: Its huge amount of total obligations and debt, the bulk of which is coming due before 2017, its relatively low and decreasing margins in comparison to its competitors, along with all the other reasons I outlined above.

I need as big of a margin of safety as possible and for the most part only value what I see in the company as it presently stands. All of the other articles I have seen have been talking about how much JACK could be worth if it spun off or sold Qdoba, or the entirety of JACK gets bought out.

To my knowledge JACK management has not said anything about spinning off Qdoba so to me valuing a company on speculation of what could happen in the future is very dangerous. I saw an article the other day where someone wrote that if Qdoba was spun off could sell for 30X EV/EBITDA because that is what Chipotle sells for. Buying any company at 30X EV/EBITDA is insane to me, especially potentially Qdoba as I do not think it has any discernible sustainable competitive advantages like Chipotle appears that it may have. I do not even know how someone would make money on that transaction, especially since Qdoba would most likely not pay any dividend as it needs to grow its store count.

Even if JACK management does decide to spin-off or sell Qdoba, the valuations and analysis that I laid out above were encompassing the entire company, and I still found JACK to be overvalued on almost every count. I do expect JACK's margins to rise over time now that the bulk of its reimaging is done, but the debt and total obligations scare me too much to be a buyer even if that happens.

Speculating is no longer what I do when investing, and to me buying into JACK now is almost purely a speculation play in the hopes that it gets bought out or spins off Qdoba. In my opinion JACK is overvalued, has no discernible moat or competitive advantages, and has some huge problems with its debt and total obligations. Combined with the rest of my above analysis, I think JACK is a bad investment.

For me personally, how I invest, what I need as a margin of safety, and the problems I outlined in the article, lead me to the conclusion that the risks far out way the pros as JACK now stands, and I will not be a buyer of it at this time.

Analysis Explanation

At this point of my value investing journey I had started to gain more confidence in my abilities to analyze a company's balance sheet and other information surrounding a company to decide if it was a good investment at the time or not. Around this time there were also more than a few articles talking about how JACK could be a great investment if it were to spin-off Qdoba.

The entire reason I started research into JACK was that an article that was written and entered by a professional investor, was one of three finalists in a value investing idea contest. All three ideas were written up very well in my opinion but I liked the one on JACK the best and ended up voting for the Jack in the Box write-up to win the contest. I thought the pro analyst laid out his investment thesis well enough that I started researching the company shortly after reading his analysis and was planning on making it an investment in my portfolio and the portfolios that I manage. The link to the professional's article can be found on my blog by searching JACK.

After doing my own research on the company I sure was glad that I now do my own full research into companies instead of just relying on what others say about a potential investment like when I started investing. It needs to be said here that every investor has different ideas of what makes a company a good investment, what kind of margin of safety they need, what risks they are willing to take, etc which are also more reasons why you must do your own research before buying into any company. You need to make sure that the company you are thinking about buying into fits YOUR particular criteria for what makes a company a good investment and not someone else's.

After I did my own research into JACK I realized that the pro investor was way too optimistic about JACK and was counting on things that MAY happen in the future. I do not even remember reading the words concern, risks, or there being any mentions of JACKs substantial debt and total obligations in his article. The write-up was almost 100% positive in favor of an investment in JACK. Every investable company has at least a few negatives lying within its financial reports so to not even mention any concerns that you have or risks that the company has or will have, means that you are either not looking in-depth enough into or that you are looking into the company and do not want to see any negatives because you are biased and want to buy into the company. Either of those scenarios is dangerous when investing real world money and is something that should be avoided at all costs. If you are not finding any negatives within a company's financial reports you need to look harder.

Overall on this topic it is important to remember the following: Do your own homework, do not listen to a bunch of hype surrounding companies even if it is from professionals, tune out the noise, and have confidence in your own investment thesis and abilities. For further discussion on this topic I recommend reading Aswath Damodaran's blog or taking his free online course where he talks about some of the biases analysts and others in the financial industry have and how you can train yourself to avoid those biases.

Combined with the above there were also other concerns I had with the professional investor's write-up that were found after doing the research and again is why you need to do your own research before buying into any company. The professional investors write-up did not mention JACK's debt and total obligations, most of which were coming due within the next five years, and did not compare JACK to its competitors at all.

Price to Book and Tangible Book Valuation:

I use a company's TTM numbers in this valuation. This is another very adaptable valuation that I use quite often when evaluating companies. Start out by multiplying the company's number of shares by its book value per share to arrive at total book value. Then subtract all intangibles, including goodwill, to arrive at the company's tangible book value. From here the structure is very similar to the Revenue and EBIT valuation.

The valuation range is similar to the FCF valuation as well because the lower percentages mean a lower valuation and the higher percentages will yield a higher valuation. Again, I use a range here with my low range usually being between 50% to 75%, mid range is usually 75% to 95%, and high range is usually 100% to 125% of the industry P/B. The range depends on many things like what I think of the company overall, how high or low the industry P/B is in relation to the companies P/B, etc. Generally only using the higher end of the range for companies that have a sustainable competitive advantage, high margins, and great profitability in relation to its competitors or if the industry P/B is extremely low.

Debt Ratios:

Being a very conservative investor I first look to make sure that there would have to have something unforeseeable happen for to lose 100% of my money and debt ratios are just one way to see if a company is financially stable. JACK's debt ratios are horrendous, especially when you count in the total obligations which are not mentioned in the company's basic balance sheet information on sites like Morningstar and are why you again need to read annual reports when doing research.

JACK's debt and total obligations is almost 22X higher than its yearly EBIT. If JACK were to have a slowdown in sales and stop growing like they were, they could have some serious trouble paying for their obligations, especially when you consider that most of its obligations were due within the next five years. The other companies that were compared above had a lot of debt but at least most of it was due after the next five years so they should not have had any immediate issues even though some of their debt loads were also excessive.

Below are explanations of what the various ratios mean. As I mentioned in the above article, Sonic had pretty good ROE and ROIC margins that were inflated by debt. Checking a company's debt levels is something you should do very quickly if the company you are researching has consistently high ROE and ROIC margins. You may have a higher tolerance for debt than me but even if you do you need to realize that if a company has a lot of debt that it will inflate its ROE and ROIC. In Sonic's case if it had a more reasonable debt load it's ROE and ROIC would have been quite a bit lower, making the company look more average in comparison when it comes to those two ratios.

Remember that I am an extremely conservative investor who generally would like to see very little debt and total obligations so the following will be what I look for when it comes to debt ratios. If you have a higher threshold for debt than I do, feel free to adjust the following to your own preferences.

- Total debt as a percentage of balance sheet: This one is pretty straight forward and is exactly like it sounds. Generally the lower the better.
- Current assets to current liabilities: Again this one is straight forward. Generally the higher the better.
- Total debt to equity: The total debt number here does not include total obligations and the equity number is shareholders equity. Generally the lower the better.
- Total debt to total assets: The total debt number here does not include total obligations. Generally the lower the better.
- Total Contractual Obligations and Commitments, Including Debt: This includes things like operating leases, capital leases, purchase commitments, debt payments, etc. These items are generally not included in the regular debt calculations, except normal short and long-term debt, and are not included in a company's balance sheet numbers that show up on sites like Morningstar and Yahoo Finance. Just the regular short and long-term debt is what shows up on the debt calculations sites like those. To illustrate this discrepancy, and the need to read annual reports again,

on Morningstar it now shows that JACK only has total short and long-term debt of $421 million. So if you were just to read financial sites and take debt information from those without looking at annual reports you are not seeing $2.2 billion in total obligations and commitments and you would think that JACK has a very healthy balance sheet. To me the total contractual obligations and commitments section of the annual report is one of the most important sections of an annual report. These kinds of recurring expenses can be a very big drain on earnings, cash flow, and profitability for years and could potentially lead to major problems at a company if they have too many of these in relation to overall profitability. Also of importance in figuring these numbers is to see when the bulk of these are coming due. In JACK's case most of them were coming due within the next five years. This was very concerning to because of the huge amount of obligations due within the next five years in relation to JACK's profitability. JACK in my opinion will not be able to pay for these obligations unless it has a huge spike in sales and profitability or it were to sell off some of its restaurants and land to pay off some of the obligations and debt. Most likely though is that JACK will have to roll over some of its debt and obligations to later years eventually by taking out more loans, likely at higher rates since interest rates are almost zero now. This could turn into a virtuous cycle of more and more debt and obligations at higher interest rates if JACK were

to not get these things under control in relation to profitability.
- Total obligations, commitments, and debt to EBIT: This is a ratio that I came up with and have never seen used anywhere else. I use this as a way to see how much total obligations, commitments, and debt a company has in relation to its yearly profitability, in this case EBIT. The higher the ratio the more debt and total obligations a company has compared to its yearly EBIT. In JACK's case its total obligations, commitments, and debt are almost 22X higher than its yearly EBIT which was shocking to me. This would lead to problems if JACK stopped growing and/or had a decline in sales in my opinion.

Comparison to Competition

After doing my own research this was another major problem I had with JACK and the professional analyst's investment thesis as he did not compare JACK to its competitors to see if its profitability ratios were better or worse than its competition. As you can see in the chapter above, JACK's ratios in comparison to its competitors are generally worse, and in some cases, a lot worse than its competition.

Combining that its ratios are generally worse than its competition with that at least on a relative valuation basis was also selling at a higher valuation when compared to its competition (Which were themselves on a relative basis selling at high valuations in comparison to other companies I evaluated and will see throughout this book) I do not see how JACK was a better buy then a lot of other companies or especially to some of its competition. McDonald's for example has generally a lot better ratios than JACK, it has competitive advantages that JACK does not, and is selling at lower relative valuations than JACK. This is crazy to me and leads me to talk about potential catalysts and the unlocking of value, which is what apparently the very bullish JACK articles and people who are buying into JACK at this point are counting on to make money.

Catalysts

Catalysts are very important to most value investors when it comes to whether to buy into a company or not and are things like: Having a valuable asset that could be spun off or sold (Like Qdoba in this case, in the case of Vivendi with its subsidiaries.

Having a lot of unused valuable land that could be sold like with Dole), emotional selling by indexes or funds that drive a company's valuations too low, a company going through a strategic review of some kind where they state that they are going to make favorable changes to a company, being bought out by another company, potential merger, a big change in the companies industry, etc.

These kinds of catalysts can unlock value and make the share price go higher and are generally sought out by value investors.

In JACK's case though the so-called catalysts that a lot of other investors saw were things that up to this point had not even been mentioned by JACK management at all, namely a potential spin-off down the road of Qdoba. The reason people think that Qdoba will eventually be spun off and make both companies share prices go higher is because of the value that was unlocked when McDonald's spun off Chipotle which it used to own. After Chipotle was spun off from McDonald's for a very good sum of money, both companies' shares rose quite a bit, and continue to rise.

The reason this is a problem when thinking that JACK could do this with Qdoba is twofold in my opinion:

1. JACK's management to my knowledge has made no mention of even thinking about spinning off Qdoba so to count on this future, unmentioned potential, in my opinion does not make any sense.

2. This is the much bigger problem of the two though. Comparing JACK and Qdoba to McDonald's and Chipotle on any level is asinine to me as both McDonald's and Chipotle have long-term sustainable competitive advantages while JACK and Qdoba do not have any kind of competitive advantages.

McDonald's spun off Chipotle to help unlock the value of both companies as McDonald's was undervalued, or at least reasonably valued, at the time of the spin-off. JACK as a whole (including Qdoba) in my opinion is overvalued, Qdoba is not as good of an asset as Chipotle, and neither Jack in the Box or Qdoba have any kind of discernible competitive advantages like McDonald's and Chipotle has.

Almost every bullish article about JACK mentioned the potential spin-off or sale of Qdoba as a reason to buy into them at the time even though JACK was not undervalued. As mentioned in the chapter above, one write-up about this "potential" on the Motley Fool even mentioned that if spun off Qdoba could sell for 30X EV/EBITDA just because that's what Chipotle was selling for at the time.

For comparison I generally like to buy companies that have an EV/EBIT under 8; EV/EBITDA equivalent is 10-12, so buying into a company at 30X EV/EBITDA is something I would never do and do not know how you would make money off that transaction unless you wanted to wait a decade while earning a very low return. As mentioned in the chapter, Qdoba would also most likely not have a dividend of any kind because it would want to continue to grow its restaurant count so you would just have to wait for the company's share value to rise to earn any kind of return.

The main lesson with catalysts is that if you do want a short to medium term catalyst in place to help unlock the value of the company you are buying is that the catalyst should make sense, be something that management has talked about, should be something that is firm that you can count on, and not be an unmentioned fantasy and hope just because another company did something that you think another company should do.

The degree that people who are bullish on JACK were relying on those unmentioned future spin-off to raise the price of its shares is crazy and will most likely lead to them losing money or having sub par investment returns with JACK in the future.

Chapter 8: Second Dole Valuation November 2012. How to Value Land, Property, and Equipment, Combining Two Different Valuations Together, and Management Issues.

"The stock market is filled with individuals who know the price of everything, but the value of nothing." Philip Fisher

Earlier this year I completely dedicated myself to learning the techniques, process, and proper mind-set to become an excellent value investor and I wrote my first full article back in June about Dole Food Company (DOLE).

To see my original Dole article and the series I did comparing it to Chiquita and Fresh Del Monte search Dole on my blog. You can also find those articles on Seeking Alpha as well. Due to its big change since my original article I have been asked by a reader what my thoughts about New Dole are now that it has eliminated what was its biggest problem; its debt. There are many articles about Dole's sale of its worldwide operations to Itochu that can be found through Google or also on my blog.

The reader wants to know what I think about New Dole's prospects going forward, if I still think the company is undervalued, or if I would think about selling now if I find it to be overvalued.

The reader also asked me about the 2009 Dole Food Automatic Common Exchange Security Trust which I talked about on my blog as well.

Since the transaction has not closed still, most of the information in the above articles remains intact as it pertains to margins and debt levels about Dole's current state. I will first value the business as I see it after the sale of its worldwide operations and then comment on what I think about New Dole's prospects after the transaction closes.

When I refer to Dole as a whole I mean Dole before the sale of its worldwide operations. New Dole is in reference to my estimates of Dole's operations after the sale of its worldwide operations. I have a call into Dole investor relations to get exact revenue and EBIT numbers for New Dole, but to this point I have not received a call back. I am estimating that New Dole will lose about 36% of its EBIT after the sale of its worldwide operations. I came to that estimate from looking at Dole's sale to Itochu presentation from September.

All numbers are in millions of U.S. dollars, except per share information, unless otherwise noted. Valuations were done using Dole's 2011 10K, second quarter and third quarter 2012 quarterly reports and presentations, and Dole's presentation of what it should look like after its asset sale.

The main thing I was worried about with any asset sale is that Dole would have to unload some of its very valuable land assets. Thankfully after the transaction is completed New Dole will still own 113,000 acres of land including some very valuable land in Hawaii. All assets below are being kept by New Dole.

Sum of the Parts Valuation

<u>Land Holdings</u>

Dole owns 25,000 acres of noncore land in Oahu valued by Dole at $500 million or $20,000 per acre. Dole also owns 22,100 acres in Costa Rica, 3,900 acres in Ecuador, and 25,500 acres in Honduras. Only part of each countries acreage are being used for growing fruit: 8,200 in Honduras, 7,300 in Costa Rica, and 3,000 in Ecuador meaning the rest could presumably be sold without interfering with current operations; about 33,000 acres.

- All Costa Rica land valued at $5,000 per acre equals $110.5 million.
- Al Ecuador land valued at $3,500 per acre equals $13.65 million.
- All Honduras land valued at $3,500 per acre equals $89.25 million.
- Remaining 36,500 acres valued at $5,000 per acre equals $182.5 million.

Adding total land value estimates up equals $895.9 million, or $7,928.32 per acre, which comes out to $10.18 per share in total land value.

Estimated value of unused non core land 33,000 acres in the above three countries at $5,000 an acre for Costa Rica and $3,500 for Honduras and Ecuador land is $75.7 million.

Total non core land assets that could be sold valued at $575.7 million total, or $9,925.86 per acre; $6.54 per share in land assets that could be sold.

Ship and Ship Related Equipment

Dole owns 13,300 refrigerated 40ft containers at a very conservative $5,000 each equal $66.5 million. This is a very conservative estimate as these containers can sell for as much as $50,000 a piece. I am using $5,000 per unit as my estimate because I want to be extra conservative and because I have not been able to find an exact break down on how many of the 13,300 container units are the 40ft refrigerated units as Dole's also has some 20ft refrigerated, and completely unrefrigerated containers, so I wanted a very conservative estimate of price to be safe.

Dole also owns 11 ships which I am very conservatively valuing at $1 million each. I found a few container ships selling for under $1 million but most were well over that price, with some reaching prices over $100 million. I am again just being conservative here because I do not have vast knowledge on the prices of Dole's ships.

Adding all the land, ship, and container value up gets us to a total of:

- All land, ship, and container value=$973.4 million, or $11.06 per share.

- Only non core land that could be sold, ship and container value=$653.2 million, or $7.42 per share.

None of Dole's operations, cash, debt, or any of its building or other equipment is counted in the above calculations. I will include Dole's cash in the below valuation.

I did not include any of its buildings or other equipment in the above valuation because I could not find any concrete information and again did not want to speculate on numbers.

Now I will value Dole's operations.

EBIT and Net Cash Valuation

Cash and cash equivalents are 82 and it has 0 in short-term investments.

Dole as a whole has a trailing twelve month EBIT of 180.7 for its entire current operations. Per Dole's sale to Itochu presentation I am estimating that it will lose about 36% of EBIT after the sale of its worldwide operations which leads to a trailing twelve month EBIT estimate of 115.65 for New Dole's operations.

5X, 8X, 11X, and 14X EBIT + cash and cash equivalents + short-term investments:

- 5X115.65=578.25+82=660.25/88=$7.50 per share.

- 8X115.65=925.2+82=1007.2/88=$11.45 per share.
- 11X115.65=1272.15+82=1354.15/88=$15.39 per share.
- 14X115.65=1619.1+82=1701.1/88=$19.33 per share.

Combined Valuation of New Dole

All values are per share values.

	Total Land, Ship, and Container Value	Only Non Core Saleable Land, Ship, and Container Value
5X EBIT	$18.56	$14.92
8X EBIT	$22.51	$18.87
11X EBIT	$26.45	$22.81
14X EBIT	$30.39	$26.75

The only thing the above values are not containing is the debt. The reason I am not including the debt in any of the estimates of intrinsic value is because Dole as a whole now has total debt of $1.4 billion but will be able to pay off all of it if it chooses to after it receives the $1.7 billion from Itochu. Thus making the above very good estimates of what New Dole should be worth after selling its worldwide operations and ridding itself of the debt.

I had an extra two paragraphs written about Dole's TEV/EBIT and ROIC margins but those had to be scrapped since I have still not heard back from Dole investor relations about New Dole's exact numbers and I did not want to speculate.

New Dole is also forecasting that after the sale is finalized it will be able to save around $100 million in cap ex and corporate expenses by the end of fiscal 2013 which supposedly are going to be yearly savings going forward, and to be able to improve its overall business operations. Even leaving improvement in operations, possible future acquisitions, and money savings out of all my calculations, New Dole should be selling at a very conservative minimum of $14.92 per share, and I actually think quite a bit higher. Current share price for the whole of Dole is $10.70 per share, a 29% margin of safety.

Dole management has also stated that after the sale to Itochu is finalized that it may look to sell or spin-off further assets, or make some acquisitions to bolster its operations within New Dole, any of which may help unlock further value in its shares. This is pure speculation, but I could see Mr. Murdock who owns around 40% of Dole, possibly looking to take the New Dole private again now that its major problem has been eliminated so he can control its operations again, which would also help unlock shareholder value.

Why after all the above has Dole as a whole been dropping in price lately? My guess is that people have sold for a combination of the following reasons:

- That Dole just released bad quarterly numbers that missed analyst estimates and which sent the herd running.
- Before that people were probably selling some personal shares that they owned to lock in profits since the stock has run up from around $8.50 a share to over $15 a share at one point.
- A lot of it may also be that people are still treating this as a highly indebted, risky, poorly operated, and marginally profitable company that it is without looking deeper at the assets that it will still hold after receiving the $1.7 billion from Itochu, and how New Dole will now be a much healthier and less risky company.

However, even if you do not count any of its operations at all, Dole as a whole is selling now for less than JUST a conservative value of the land, ship, and containers that it owns. Meaning the downside is covered by hard saleable assets even if New Dole's operations were to become massively unprofitable, which I think is very unlikely.

New Dole looks to be massively undervalued, will still hold very good high value assets, especially saleable land, has some future potential catalysts that could help unlock value, it should be able to compete better with Fresh Del Monte and Chiquita, and New Dole will now be freed up to make acquisitions and improvements to its business and operations after the transaction with Itochu closes as it will not be burdened by the massive amount of debt that it has carried for years.

I plan to buy shares for my personal account and add more shares back into the accounts I manage after selling some Dole shares up 70% in September.

Analysis Explanation:

The EBIT and cash valuation by this point should be very familiar but just to reiterate again that valuation only contains the companies operating income, cash, and short-term investments. For a situation like with Dole directly above, and Vivendi earlier in the book, with companies who either own a lot of land, property, and equipment, or are more or a less a holding company/conglomerate like Vivendi the sum of the parts valuation is very useful. Sum of the parts valuations are very simple and straight forward as you just add together all the disparate parts of a company to find an estimated value of its assets.

Do not be deceived by the simplicity however as the sum of the parts valuations generally take the most time to do of any of the valuation techniques in this book. Especially if the value of all the company's property, land, and equipment are not publicly listed as was the case with Dole. When doing a sum of the parts valuation try to find at least two sources that can give estimated values of some of the items.

As talked about a bit in the article, ship and the refrigerated container prices seemed to vary by quite a bit based on a lot of different factors, and since I have very little knowledge about those things was as conservative as possible in the estimates. It was relatively easy to find estimated value of an acre of land where Dole owned land but it was far more time-consuming to find information on some of the ships that Dole owned. As always, being a very conservative investor I generally always use the most conservative value of the assets that are found.

Putting the two above valuations together is something I came up with and have seen no one else do before but it made sense to me in this situation and a few others. To me it did not make sense in this situation to keep the operations and cash of the company separate from the land and equipment value. Another reason I did the above was because Dole was getting paid more than what it had in total debt. If this wasn't the case and Dole for example would have only made $1 billion from the sale to Itochu, I would have subtracted the remaining total debt amount (In this case about $400 million) from the valuations which is what you should do if you come across a situation like that.

Also of note in the article was the 2009 Dole Food Automatic Common Exchange Security Trust which I explained as best as possible on my blog from information found online. If you are interested in broadening your knowledge and learning about a complex uncommon situation I recommend searching for the blog post about the security trust transaction.

Update

As I have been writing, editing, and revising this book, Dole's Chairman Mr. Murdock has put in an offer to take the company private once again so I wanted to write my thoughts on the ridiculous offer being given to Dole shareholders. I thought that Mr. Murdock may have wanted to take the company private again but what I didn't expect was the manipulation of the company's stock price in my opinion before that happened. Shortly after Dole sold its worldwide operations to Itochu Dole management began to do some very strange things. The value of its land holdings, that Dole management themselves estimated to be worth around $500 million when they were getting ready to sell their worldwide operations to Itochu, suddenly stated that they thought their land now was worth only around $250 million only a few months later.

This was shocking and led to me sell the stock I owned in Dole in my personal portfolio and the portfolios that I manage because I figured that Dole was doing something untoward to try to get the value of its shares down so the company could be taken private again at a cheaper valuation. One of my followers on Seeking Alpha and I actually talked about this and both came to the same conclusion that something fishy was going on.

After selling my shares in Dole due to the above situation I stopped paying attention to the company all together to concentrate on the research of other companies until it came out that Dole was planning to do a massive buyback of its shares. This was a very good thing for them to do since I found the company to be very undervalued when writing my second article on them so I started to look into them a little bit again. Before I could do even minimal research into the new situation at Dole its management made another very strange decision. A few days after Dole announced that it was going to buy back $200 million worth of its shares it changed its mind and all of a sudden decided to update its fleet of container ships instead and canceled the proposed share buyback program.

Of course this sent the share price falling and again led me to believe that its management was trying to manipulate the share price lower so that it could be taken private at an unreasonably low valuation.

Unfortunately it turns out that I seem to have been right because a month or two after Dole decided to cancel its proposed share buyback program to instead buy new container ships, which of course sent the share price lower, Mr. Murdock announced that he was putting in an offer to take Dole private at $12 a share.

Mr. Murdock brought Dole public in 2009 at $12.50 a share so this in and of itself is ridiculous since the company is much more financially stable now than it was then due to getting rid of its giant debt load. In my opinion this entire situation from the changing of the estimated value of its land by 50% shortly after announcing that they thought it was worth $500 million, announcing the proposed $200 million share buyback and then a few days later canceling it, and then Mr. Murdock attempting to take the company private again at an incredibly low valuation should be investigated. If Dole is allowed to be taken private at $12 a share, which it probably will because Mr. Murdock at my last check still owned 40% of the company, then the company should be investigated for manipulating its stock price by the SEC. If the company is taken private for a paltry $12 per share then its remaining shareholders are getting screwed.

If a situation like this happens to a company you own be very careful, trust your research, trust your instincts, and get out of owning the company if you think you need to. There are many other companies you can spend your time researching and owning rather than spending your precious time and capital having to worry about whether a company's management is going to screw over shareholders. Dole's current shareholders are fighting back by suing the company and I wish them good luck because the proposed buyout offer is ridiculously low.

Chapter 9: Wendy's (WEN) November 2012. TEV/EBIT, Relative Valuations, Management Issues, Cap Ex, Share Buybacks, Contrarian, and Negative Equity and Book Values.

"Investing should be more like watching paint dry or watching grass grow. If you want excitement, take $800 and go to Las Vegas." Paul Samuelson

About a month and a half ago I wrote an article stating that I believe Jack in the Box to be overvalued despite the recent positive hype around the company. Lately I have researched Wendy's because it has had JACK's opposite problem; very negative recent press and wanted to see if this might turn out to be a potential contrarian value play or a value trap.

I will be referring to and comparing Wendy's to Jack In The Box and the other fast food companies I wrote about in my JACK article so if you would like to see how Wendy's compares to other fast food companies please reference my JACK article that I link to above.

Wendy's Overview

Wendy's is an owner, operator, and franchiser of 6,543 fast food restaurants, 1,447 of the restaurants are owned directly by Wendy's with the remaining amount owned by franchisees. Wendy's offers hamburgers, chicken sandwiches, salads, wraps, fries, and the rest of the typical fast food restaurant offerings but at a higher quality profile than most of its other fast food competitors. Higher quality also leads to higher prices for its individual product offerings and meals which greatly affected the company during the recession with customers generally looking for cheaper food. In the past several years to combat the low-cost offerings of its competitors, Wendy's has brought out its own value and extra value menus with prices generally under $2 per item.

Since the recession Wendy's has streamlined operations by selling off its Arby's subsidiary, enacting cost cutting measures, updating its menu to offer new products including breakfast at some locations, and has started reimaging some of its restaurants by starting its Image Activation Program. The program has been put into place to update its restaurants making them look more modern, offering more amenities to get customers to stay longer at its restaurants, and making the food ordering and cooking process more efficient so customers can get their food faster.

Unlike JACK who has recently finished up its reimaging of its restaurants and who should see at least small margin growth due to lower capital expenditures, Wendy's has only just started this process with only a few dozen restaurants having been updated thus far. Wendy's hopes that by 2015 about half of its company owned restaurants will be reimaged so this process is going to take a while. As we saw with Jack In The Box that will lead to generally higher cap ex for the foreseeable future, most likely lower or stagnant margins, possibly more debt, and potential loss of sales due to having some of its restaurants closed for construction periods of as long as eight weeks now.

Valuations

All numbers are in millions of US dollars, except per share information, unless otherwise noted. The following valuations were done using its 2011 10K, 3Q 2012 10Q, and its 3Q 2012 investor presentation slides.

Asset Reproduction Valuation

Assets:	Book Value:	Reproduction Value:
Current Assets		
Cash And Cash Equivalents	454	454
Accounts Receivable (Net)	65	55
Inventories	12	8
Prepaid Expenses & Other Current Assets	32	16
Deferred Income Tax Benefit	95	48
Advertising Funds Restricted Assets	75	50
Total Current Assets	734	631
Properties	1241	745
Goodwill	877	439

Other Intangible Assets	1315	658
Investments	118	89
Deferred Costs & Other Assets	57	29
Total Assets	4340	2591

Number of shares are 390

Reproduction Value:

With goodwill and intangible assets:

- 2591/390=$6.64 per share.

Without goodwill and intangible assets:

- 1494/390=$3.83 per share.

EBIT and Net Cash Valuation

Cash and cash equivalents are 454

Short term investments are 0

Total current liabilities are 344

Number of shares are 390

Cash and cash equivalents + short-term investments - total current liabilities=454-344=110.

- 110/390=$0.28 in net cash per share.

WEN has a trailing twelve month EBIT of 120.

5X, 8X, 11X, and 14X EBIT + cash and cash equivalents + short-term investments:

- 5X120=600+454=1054/390=$2.70 per share.
- 8X120=960+454=1414/390=$3.63 per share.
- 11X120=1320+454=1774/390=$4.55 per share.
- 14X120=1680+454=2134/390=$5.47 per share.

TEV/EBIT and EV/EBIT Valuation

Total enterprise value is market cap + all debt equivalents (including the capitalized value of operating leases, unfunded pension liability, etc) – cash - long-term investments - net deferred tax assets.

- TEV/EBIT=3310/120=27.58
- TEV/EBIT without accumulated deficit counted=2833/120=23.61
- Regular EV/EBIT=2946/120=24.55

The average EV/EBIT in the fast food industry that I found when analyzing JACK was 15.68 and the only company to have a higher EV/EBIT than Wendy's is Chipotle Mexican Grill $CMG which had an EV/EBIT of 26.53.

I usually like to buy companies that have an EV/EBIT multiple under 8 so the fast food industry as a whole appears to be massively overvalued to me. Not only that but Wendy's current EV/EBIT multiple is comparable to Chipotle's which generally has very high margins, and is exactly the opposite case from Wendy's. As we will see later Wendy's margins do not even come close to Chipotle's and are generally much worse than even the rest of the fast food companies margins, so it's extraordinarily high EV/EBIT multiple is astounding and I will explain later why it is so high.

I also did my normal other valuations but they did not work because after you take out the company's debt and/or goodwill and intangibles from the other valuations you get negative estimates of intrinsic value for Wendy's equity.

Margin comparison

Please reference my JACK article above to see my thoughts on the other company's margins as I will only be commenting in this article about Wendy's margins. The below chart has been updated to include Wendy's margins for comparison to the other fast food companies. The industry averages are still only including the earlier five companies I talked about.

	Jack in the Box (JACK)	Sonic Corp (SONC)	McDonald's (MCD)	Yum Brands (YUM)	Chipotle Mexican Grill (CMG)	Company Averages	Wendy's (WEN)
Gross Margin 5 Year Average	16.28%	34.30%	37.94%	26.20%	24.28%	27.80%	25.70%
Gross Margin 10 Year Average	17.08%	43.38%	40.42%	35.59%	11.73%	29.04%	39.86%
Op Margin 5 Year Average	7.46%	16.24%	27.42%	14.22%	12.76%	15.62%	-1.70%
Op Margin 10 Year Average	7.07%	18.05%	22.62%	13.50%	6.64%	13.57%	0.21%
ROE 5 Year Average	20.16%	66.33%	30.26%	131.56%	18.55%	53.37%	-6%
ROE 10 Year Average	18.77%	43.71%	23.19%	105.85%	10.27%	40.36%	-4.68%
ROIC 5 Year Average	11.17%	3.38%	17.38%	24.97%	18.49%	15.08%	-3.77%
ROIC 10 Year Average	10.91%	8.97%	13.37%	23.54%	10.22%	13.40%	-2.45%
FCF/Sales 5 Year Average	-0.26%	6.48%	15.90%	7.70%	6.92%	7.35%	1.07%
FCF/Sales 10 Year Average	0.80%	7.10%	12.86%	6.70%	2.26%	5.94%	-3.74%
Cash Conversion Cycle 5 Year Average	0.78	1.23	0.91	-36.35	-5.24	-7.92	-4.18
Cash Conversion Cycle 10 Year Average	0.27	1.14	-1.22	-49.02	-5.21	-10.81	-4.53

P/B Current	2.9	12.4	6.7	14.3	8.2	8.9	0.9
Insider Ownership Current	0.38%	6.12%	0.07%	0.50%	1.64%	1.74%	6.83%
EV/EBIT Current	14.25	9.65	12.16	15.81	26.53	15.68	24.55
Debt Comparisons:							
Total Debt as a % of Balance Sheet 5 year Average	30.78%	80.91%	35.28%	45.24%	0	38.44%	34.03%
Total debt as a % of Balance Sheet 10 year Average	26.84%	50.77%	35.22%	40.72%	0.14%	30.74%	38.58%
Current Assets to Current Liabilities	1.02	1.38	1.24	0.97	4.13	1.75	2.13
Total Debt to Equity	1.03	9.69	0.97	1.6	0	2.66	0.81
Total Debt to Total Assets	30.50%	71.20%	41%	37.21%	0	35.98%	36.87%
Total Contractual Obligations and Commitments, Including Debt	$2.6 Billion	$1 Billion	$27.20 Billion	$11.42 Billion	$2.20 Billion	$8.88 Billion	$1.9 Billion
Total Obligations and Debt/EBIT	21.67	8.85	3.15	5.4	5.82	8.98	13.33

All numbers in the table were put together using either Morningstar or Yahoo Finance.

As you can see from the above margin comparison, Wendy's margins are almost all quite a bit worse or at best about even with industry averages in comparison to its fast food competitors. Even if we were to exclude Wendy's absolutely horrible 2008 from its numbers, its margins are still quite a bit lower than its competitors.

Especially of note are the horrible in comparison to its competitor's margins: ROIC, ROE, FCF/Sales, EV/EBIT, and Total obligations and debt/EBIT ratios, which are all a lot worse than its competitor's ratios. Wendy's EV/EBIT is especially inflated due to its high amount of debt in comparison to its profitability which is why it has a comparable EV/EBIT to the much higher margin Chipotle.

My calculations of ROIC are a bit different from Morningstar's numbers and help out Wendy's a bit, but even at 5.4% without goodwill and 3.85% with goodwill those numbers are still generally quite inferior to its competitors.

About the only thing that Wendy's has in favor for itself out of the entire above table is that its P/B ratio of 0.9 is a lot lower than its competitors. A P/B ratio that low generally means that the company could be undervalued. That P/B ratio in this case is a bit of a farce because goodwill and other intangible assets make up the vast majority of current book value as just those two combine for an estimated $2.2 billion in value. After subtracting goodwill and intangible assets tangible book value is actually negative. The $2.2 billion is actually more than the current market cap so I think that it is fair to say that those values are probably massively overstated and may soon have to be restated or written down to a more reasonable level, thus eliminating some further perceived value and bringing the P/B value up closer to its competitors.

I also think that Wendy's debt levels and costs are too high in comparison to its profitability as 83% of operating profit (EBIT) goes to interest expenses. Costs and other expenses, not including interest expense and loss on extinguishment of debt, take up 95% of total sales. Other expenses include general and administrative, depreciation and amortization, etc. If you include interest expenses and loss on extinguishment of debt that takes total costs and expenses over 100% of sales, which is why Wendy's recent earnings have been negative.

Pros

- Pays a dividend and recently upped it 100%.
- After a lot of the stores are reimaged margins should improve due to lower cap ex and higher same store sales. Of the stores that have thus far been reimaged Wendy's says they have seen 25% increases in sales.
- Has positive net cash.
- Has a good amount of cash on hand.
- Same store sales have risen for 6 straight quarters and a total of 2.3% in the past 9 months.
- Wendy's has recently paid off some of its 10% coupon debt by taking out lower interest debt, which should lead to lower interest expenses going forward.
- Wendy's recently overtook Burger King as the second biggest fast food burger chain.
- Owns a lot of its restaurants and the property underneath the buildings so Wendy's does hold

- some valuable assets for when it has some problems.
- Just fewer than 80% of its restaurants are owned by franchisees that pay a 4% royalty to Wendy's. Collecting franchise royalty fees is a very high margin business.
- The company produces positive FCF excluding cap ex.

Cons

- Wendy's is overvalued by every one of my valuations, sometimes in extreme cases, except when including the massive amount of goodwill and intangible assets.
- Wendy's margins overall are generally a lot worse than its fast food competitors.
- Book value is only positive because of goodwill and other intangible assets.
- The company has had recent negative earnings.
- 83% of operating profit went to interest expense.
- The company's equity has negative value after subtracting goodwill and intangible assets on various valuations.
- The company has bought back a lot of stock at what I think are overvalued prices.
- The company's debt levels and costs are too high in my opinion in comparison to its profitability levels.
- Wendy's will have higher cap ex for the foreseeable future due to the reimagining of its stores.

- The reimaging of Wendy's stores could be going on for at least a decade if not more as it hopes to have around 750 stores reimaged by 2015 leaving around 5,750 stores to be reimaged after that, not including new stores that are opened by Wendy's itself or its franchisees.
- Cap ex this year has been around $225 million and will likely stay close to that elevated level for many years due to the reimagining of its stores and which should either lead to lowering or stagnating margins for the foreseeable future.
- The company has negative FCF when including cap ex.
- This year the company spent $126 million in cash on cap ex with the remaining $99 million coming from other sources. To me that means Wendy's will have to either increase its margins and FCF to pay the remaining cap ex costs, or more likely it will continue to have to issue debt to fund the reimaging of its stores.
- While sales have risen within Wendy's, costs have also been rising at about the same amount which is why margins have not been increasing much as sales have improved.
- The company has quite a few, what seem to me questionable compensation and related party transactions within the company, including with Mr. Peltz (former Wendy's executive and current chairman) and Trian Partners the investment fund Mr. Peltz has formed with a couple Wendy's other board members.
- Just one example of the questionable transactions is that Wendy's paid just under $640,000 in

security costs for Mr. Peltz who is a billionaire and could easily pay these costs himself.
- Trian Partners now owns just under 25% of Wendy's and has three members on Wendy's board of directors so Trian could exert a lot of pressure on Wendy's if it saw fit to do so.
- Due to some of what seem to me to be questionable transactions; I do not trust management to do what is right for shareholders and to increase shareholder value.

Potential Catalysts

- The reimaging of its stores will most likely eventually lead to margin and sales growth.
- If Wendy's can get its costs under control, which it is trying to do now, it could achieve some margin growth.
- In my opinion Wendy's has overstated its goodwill and other intangible assets and may have to restate or write down some of the value of each. Wendy's warns it may have to do this in its most recent annual report, which would lead to less perceived value in the company, and would probably drop the price of the stock further.

Conclusion

Wendy's has recently overtaken the number two spot for hamburger fast food chains in the United States from Burger King. Growth in this case appears to be bad for shareholders as its costs have risen about in line with sales which are why margins have not seen much growth as Wendy's sales have grown. Wendy's margins are also generally quite a bit worse than its other fast food competitors, in my opinion its debt levels and costs are too high, and I do not trust its management to do what is right for shareholders.

Wendy's appears to be destroying shareholder value with its high costs and debt levels, buying back its stock at overvalued prices, and continuing to grow its restaurant count and sales but not improving its margins. Because Wendy's margins have not improved as sales have risen, it looks like Wendy's is growing at less than its cost of capital which in my opinion has led to value destruction for shareholders. The destruction of shareholder value will not reverse unless Wendy's can cut its costs and debt levels and or improve profitability which probably will not happen for a while due to some of the reasons stated above. Unless something drastic happens, in my opinion shareholders of Wendy's stock can only look forward to further value destruction of their shares into the future.

Having stated all the above I would estimate Wendy's intrinsic value to be my 5X EBIT and cash valuation of $2.70 per share. Due to all of what I stated in the above article I do not think that Wendy's is even worth its reproduction value and I would not even be a buyer of the company at my $2.70 per share estimate of value.

Even if Wendy's margins and sales do rise after reimaging of its stores, which should happen, that will not take place for many years as Wendy's has only recently started to reimage its restaurants.

I hope I am wrong about Wendy's because food wise it is by far my favorite fast food restaurant where I live. I hope it can fix its problems, and hope that it starts to thrive as a company. However, as an investment I think Wendy's is the proverbial value trap and I plan to keep my investment funds far away from the company.

Analysis Explanation:

Going into researching Wendy's I was thinking that because of some of the factors that were listed in the above chapter that it may be a potential contrarian value play. It was pretty shunned and not thought of very highly in the investment world. Being a very contrarian person I automatically was thinking that because this was a relatively shunned company that this would be an opportunity to find an undervalued and unloved company that people were just missing out on.

It turns out that being contrarian for contrarian sake is not always a good idea and that you need to keep an open mind when researching companies, especially if you are a very contrarian person and want to run against the herd. Turns out most everyone was right about Wendy's as it turned out to be a very indebted, poorly run, and unshareholder friendly company.

The company is very indebted, especially when considering total obligations and commitments, and it looks like it will have to continue to issue debt as it does not make enough money to sustain the restaurant reimaging initiative by itself as the company has negative earnings when counting interest on its debt payments. Wendy's has had a decent history of dividends and doing share buybacks but even these normally positive things are negatives when it comes to Wendy's.

Normally people who do research into a company look for companies that issue dividends and buyback shares. In this case both are awful for Wendy's and this is one of the things that I improved on from the JACK evaluation. In the chapter on JACK I stated that the company had bought back its shares recently and that was a good thing. Red from the Red Corner Blog commented on my JACK article on my blog and pointed out that I was wrong about JACK buying back its shares being a good thing. Normally it is but only if the company buys back shares when the company is undervalued. If the company's management buys back shares when a company is overvalued then its management is destroying value most of the time like in the cases of JACK and Wendy's. The dividends issue here is a matter of opinion more so than the buyback issue and in my opinion Wendy's would be much better served by stopping the dividend and using that money to pay off debt as Wendy's is actually mildly profitable when not including the interest on the company's debt.

There would be some backlash here from shareholders if they were to stop the dividends, but it would be for the overall betterment of the company in the long run. The more egregious of the two issues though is that Wendy's has been continuing to do share buybacks when the company is overvalued.

To maximize shareholder value generally the rule of thumb is that when a company is overvalued you are supposed to issue shares, and take the money from that transaction to help grow the company, pay down debt, whatever. Generally when you want to buy back shares is when a company is undervalued to lower the number of shares to make each share worth more and to raise EPS. If you invert those general rules you are at best minimizing shareholder value or at worst, and in the case of Wendy's, destroying value within the company. Unfortunately, the latter is the way most companies do things and very few companies get this principle right.

Worst of all though is that because Wendy's doesn't make enough money to sustain the dividend, buybacks, and restaurant reimaging on its own is that it will have to continue to issue more and more debt to sustain the current status quo. Unless there is a change in the previous policies, Wendy's shareholders will have the value of their equity investments continued to be destroyed while profitability continues to deteriorate further.

Wendy's spent a total of $225 million on cap ex in 2012 (Or almost 2X EBIT), most from cash, and the rest from other sources as I said above. If you spend almost 2X EBIT on cap ex, and this isn't even including other costs or taxes remember, then you will continue to get further and further into debt. The other sources line is most likely Wendy's having to issue more debt. Most of this cap ex was related to the reimaging of restaurants which will continue for years. What Wendy's is doing is unsustainable in my eyes and do not think that they can continue to spend all that money on cap ex, dividends, share buy backs, and the reimaging of its stores without having to continue to issue more and more debt or by somehow lowering costs and improving profitability pretty drastically.

Valuation, Growth, Ratios, and Etc Issues

Wendy's is in a very similar boat that JACK was in the earlier chapter about them. JACK's problems were that it was about fairly valued or overvalued at the time and that its margins, debt, profitability, and other ratios are about on par or worse than its competitors. Wendy's problems are a lot worse than even JACK's as it is a lot less profitable, it has more debt as a percentage of the balance sheet, its margins and ratios are generally worse than the industry average by far, most are worse than JACK's, and Wendy's is overvalued on an intrinsic and relative valuation basis with almost every one of my valuations.

The previous myriad of things does not even include that JACK has recently finished up the reimaging of its stores and should see some margin improvement from the lowering of those restaurant improvement related costs. Wendy's has just started the reimaging of its restaurants and should see some margin decline or stagnation over time due to those costs which could lead to further deterioration of profitability. The only company in the fast food industry that has a higher valuation on a relative basis than Wendy's is Chipotle which is a great deal more profitable than Wendy's. On an EV/EBIT basis, Wendy's is by far the highest valued company using that metric which is shocking considering how low its margins generally are and how low its profitability is.

Also of major note here is that generally growth is considered good for a company as it brings in more revenue, potentially more market share, possible margin growth, greater brand recognition, etc. In Wendy's case however as the company has grown its sales and market share (It recently overtook Burger King as the number two fast food burger chain in the US) it has come at the cost of destroying shareholder value by constantly having to issue more and more debt to sustain current operations and company policy.

If Wendy's was growing in a healthy and efficient way than its margins would be seeing some improvement as it was growing its restaurant count, it would be improving its profitability while lowering costs, and it would not have to continually issue debt just to continue operations and company policy as they are.

Director Compensation and Related Party Transactions

The following quoted areas are direct quotes from Wendy's 2012 Proxy and are things that as an investor made me very uncomfortable and make it seem that Wendy's management does not have its shareholders best interests at heart.

"For Mr. Peltz, also reflects security-related costs paid by the Company during fiscal 2011. In connection with Mr. Peltz' service as non-executive Chairman, and as a result of the Company's review of certain security issues, the Board of Directors has approved payments for certain security services, security personnel and residential security equipment provided to Mr. Peltz and members of his immediate family. The aggregate amount of such security-related costs paid by the Company during fiscal 2011 was $638,911."

As an extremely conservative value investor I want management to be looking out for shareholders when it comes to their decisions and use of capital, and I want to be able to trust that management has its shareholders' best interests at heart. Even if there are or were security threats as it pertains to Mr. Peltz, the man is a billionaire and could easily pay those costs himself. It is not a huge amount of money but to me a cost like that shows that management does not have shareholders best interests at heart. I might add that this is the first time I have seen anything like that in all the annual and proxy reports I have read.

There are also two related party transactions that made me uneasy.

1. Aircraft Agreement. In June 2009, the Company and TASCO, LLC ("TASCO"), an affiliate of Trian Partners, entered into an aircraft lease agreement, which provided that the Company would lease a corporate aircraft to TASCO from July 1, 2009 to June 30, 2010. In June 2010, the term of the lease agreement was renewed for an extra one-year period, expiring June 30, 2011. Under the lease agreement TASCO paid $10,000 per month, plus substantially all operating costs of the aircraft, including all costs of fuel, inspection, servicing and certain storage, as well as operational and flight crew costs relating to the operation of the aircraft, and all transit maintenance costs and other maintenance costs required as a result of TASCO's usage of the aircraft.

The Company remained responsible for calendar-based maintenance and any extraordinary and unscheduled repairs and/or maintenance for the aircraft, as well as insurance and other costs. In June 2011, the term of the lease agreement was extended for an additional one-year period, expiring June 30, 2012, with an increased monthly rent of $13,000. The lease agreement may be terminated by the Company without penalty in the event the Company sells the aircraft to a third party, subject to a right of first refusal in favor of Trian Partners with respect to such a sale. The Company intends to dispose of the aircraft as soon as practicable. The Company received $138,000 from Trian Partners under the lease agreement for 2011.

I remember reading in some of the documents that were read while researching the original article on Wendy's something to the effect that wives of executives could ride on the private jet with the executives, if the wives had business in the city the plane was going to, and that executives were not supposed to use the plane for personal use. I remember that it did not explicitly bar executives from using the planes for personal use. Those are not direct quotes and I may have misremembered the exact wording but those statements bothered me enough that I still remember them today.

2. *Liquidation Services Agreement. In June 2009, the Company and Trian Partners entered into a liquidation services agreement, which expired on June 30, 2011.*
 Pursuant to the liquidation services agreement, Trian Partners assisted the Company in the sale, liquidation or other disposition of certain investments that were not related to the Company's core restaurant business. In consideration for these services, the liquidation services agreement required the Company to pay Trian Partners a fee of $900,000 in two installments: (i) $450,000 upon signing the agreement; and (ii) $450,000 on June 30, 2010.

Again just for perception sake couldn't they have found someone else to do this same business with?

I would not characterize any of the above as egregious or illegal, but as a value investor who digs very deep into company filings, and needs be able to trust that management has its shareholders' best interests at heart, the above made me uneasy and make it seem that management is not looking out for shareholders best interests. Along with some of the other things written about in this chapter I was not able to trust management enough at Wendy's to be a buyer into the company, even if the company was undervalued enough for me to consider that transaction which they of course were not.

As a side note it seems that Mr. Peltz and Mr. May, both members of Trian, are on the committees that had to approve the above transactions that were bothersome.

The above information is why you must read proxy reports as well as annual and quarterly reports. The proxy report details things like executive and director compensation, how they are compensated, related party transactions, who owns 5% and above of the company's shares, etc.

Combining the above overvaluation, buying back shares when shares are overvalued, growing inefficiently, the continued issuing of debt, destroying of shareholder value in my opinion, and the director compensation and related party transaction issues that bothered me, I do not believe that Wendy's management has shareholders best interests at heart and to me this is a very good example of a value trap.

New Terms

The next term was learned from Red over at the Red Corner Blog. This is another one of those rare sources of outstanding information that is highly recommended for everyone to visit.

I recommend going back to the beginning of his blog and reading everything while also taking notes. If you do it is guaranteed that you will learn a lot, more than most other sites that I have found put together. He is also very good at answering questions from readers so if you have any specific questions make sure to ask them in any of the comments sections on his blog postings.

Total Enterprise Value (TEV) - Market cap + all debt equivalents (including the capitalized value of operating leases, generally at 7X, unfunded pensions, etc) - cash, cash equivalents, and short-term investments - long-term investments - net deferred tax assets. This gives a much truer look at the company and its debt situation as all debt equivalents are included: Future and recurring purchase agreements, leases, pensions, rent/mortgage obligations, future commitments, and future obligations. This has become one of my favorites and is something I look at with every company I research.

TEV/EBIT- This is using the total enterprise value/operating margin instead of the regular enterprise value/operating margin that we talked about before. As with EV/EBIT I generally like to see this value of 8 and below when thinking about buying into a company. This ratio along with my calculations of ROIC and a few other ratios and metrics are my favorites to use when evaluating a company and are given great weight when considering whether to buy into a company.

Negative tangible book value - This can happen if a company has a lot of debt, goodwill, and intangible assets like Wendy's. Generally I do not like to see this, especially if it is due to debt and goodwill. These assets are a drag on profitability in the case of debt, or just purely an accounting number that has little to no effect on how a company truly operates as in the case of goodwill most of the time. If it is due to intangible assets (Things like patents, trademarks, customer lists, non-compete agreements, etc) this is not as much of a bad thing, and can actually be a potentially very valuable hidden asset. I still do not count on these so-called intangibles as much as with hard saleable assets like land and buildings but that is just a personal preference.

Negative equity value-Pretty much the same as above and can happen if a company has a lot of debt, goodwill, and intangible assets. This is worse though because if the only "true" value in the company is what management deems intangibles and debt, especially if most of the so-called value is due to debt and goodwill, then you may have some problems. For example, after subtracting all of Wendy's debt, goodwill, and intangible assets Wendy's equity actually has a negative value meaning that is worth less than zero.

This means that the only true value at Wendy's currently is within the company's debt, goodwill, and intangible assets. Wendy's business is not producing enough value within its actual operations and has to rely on the continued issuing of debt. It is most likely listing the book value i.e. (not true economic value) of its goodwill and intangible assets on its balance sheet at too optimistic of a value. This can be seen from Wendy's own 10K where they say that the value of goodwill and intangible assets may have to be written down or written off in the future which would destroy value within the company and drop its share price.

In the next chapter we will detail a company in the same fast food industry as JACK and Wendy's that has grown in a very healthy and efficient way. I urge you to come back to the chapters about JACK and Wendy's to compare them to Brazil Fast Food Company (BOBS) that will be outlined in the next chapter so you can see the amazing differences between how the companies run, their profitability, and how management has run the three different companies so you get a good idea of how a company should be operated in the fast food industry.

Chapter 10: Brazil Fast Food (BOBS) December 2012. How To Calculate ROIC, Great Management, Competitive Advantages, Net Operating Loss Carry Forwards (NOL's), Relative Valuations, and OTC and Pink Sheet Companies.

"Have the courage of your knowledge and experience. If you have formed a conclusion from the facts and if you know your judgment is sound, act on it - even though others may hesitate or differ. You are neither right nor wrong because the crowd disagrees with you. You are right because your data and reasoning are right." Benjamin Graham

In this chapter I will be talking about Brazil Fast Food Company (BOBS.OB). Bob's was founded in 1952 by

American tennis player Bob Falkenberg and serves hamburgers and sandwiches with a Brazilian twist, shakes, French fries, and other typical fast food offerings. BOBS has grown to become the second biggest fast food chain in Brazil with operations in every state of the country, Angola, and Chile.

When I talk about BOBS in all capital letters I mean the company as a whole. When I refer to Bob's it means just the fast food burger chain.

A fellow value investor mentioned on my blog that I should research BOBS as a possible investment since I have already researched and written articles on a couple fast food companies; Jack in the Box (JACK) and Wendy's (WEN). Also with my recent turn towards concentrating on micro caps he thought I might find this company interesting.

I have found BOBS to be very interesting and it has turned into only the fifth company I have bought into this year as it meets most of my criteria for things I look for in a potential investment. Some main points of interest are: I have found BOBS to be substantially undervalued, I believe BOBS to have a competitive advantage, or moat that has grown in the past several years, the company is very small and under followed, and its sales and margins have also been growing in recent years.

Introduction

For the better part of the last 60 years Brazil Fast Food has been operating and franchising only its Bob's fast food burger chain and expanding the chains reach throughout Brazil. The following link contains a very good history of BOBS up to 2004 that goes over its many struggles and near death multiple times: http://www.answers.com/topic/brazil-fast-food-corp Very interesting read especially when you consider what they have become now. After updating its stores, changing the Bob's logo, enacting cost cutting and efficiency measures, and changing its strategy to become a multi-brand restaurant company with partnerships to bring KFC and Pizza Hut restaurants to Brazil, and through acquiring Doggi's and Yoggi's, BOBS has expanded its restaurant count dramatically and expanded from just selling burgers, sandwiches, shakes, and fries, into selling KFC's chicken related products, pizza's, hot dogs, frozen yogurt and smoothies to become the second largest fast food chain in Brazil.

As we found out in the chapter on Wendy's, growth is not always a good thing if your cost of capital is very high due to debt and other costs. Luckily BOBS debt is at a very manageable level and BOBS has lowered its costs over the last few years. The growth in the amount and type of products along with the growing restaurant count has helped grow revenues and margins at pretty substantial percentages over the last several years. Most importantly of all, I believe BOBS is growing at less than its cost of capital because as it has grown its store count and sales it has become more profitable.

Also helping to grow BOBS as a whole is that I believe that it has at least some minor competitive advantages which it has had for a while now but has only recently been fully unleashed due to BOBS growing scale as it pertains to its growing number of restaurants, and its cost cutting and efficiency measures over the last several years. At this point I cannot say for certain whether the small moat I see for BOBS is sustainable for the long-term, but this is the first company I have evaluated in a while where I see a very clear moat.

Overview of Operations and Subsidiaries

Before 2007, Brazil Fast Food Company just consisted of Bob's burger chain which I described above. In 2007 BOBS as a whole started on its path towards becoming a multi-brand restaurant operation as it agreed with Yum Brands (YUM) to open KFC restaurants in Brazil. In 2009 BOBS further expanded to include operating some Pizza Hut's in Brazil and it also acquired Doggi's hot dog chain. In 2012 BOBS further expanded as it acquired Yoggi's frozen yogurt and smoothie company. Since its beginnings as a regional company in Brazil with the bulk of its operations in the Southeastern portion of the country, BOBS has grown into the second biggest fast food chain in Brazil behind only McDonald's (MCD) with operations in every state in Brazil. BOBS has also started to grow outside of Brazil as it now has operations in Chile and Angola.

Below is a chart showing how BOBS has grown its restaurant count since 2007.

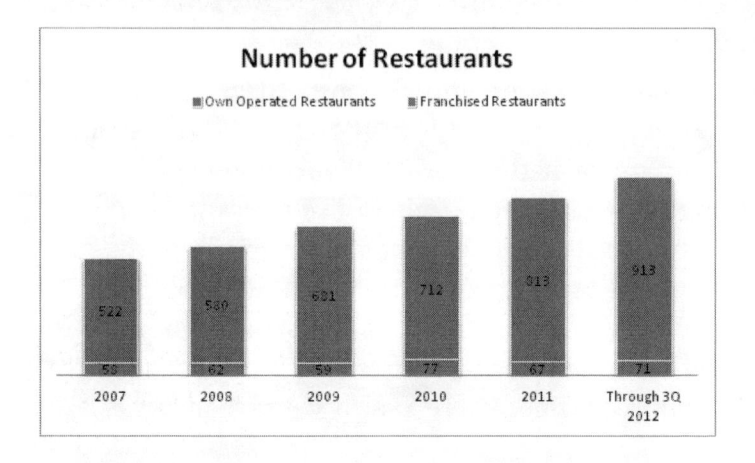

Number of Restaurants

Year	Own Operated Restaurants	Franchised Restaurants
2007	53	522
2008	62	580
2009	59	681
2010	77	712
2011	67	813
Through 3Q 2012	71	913

Restaurant count has grown by 7% annually since 2007. Its growing size and now countrywide operations have enabled BOBS to sign some very favourable agreements with suppliers. Here are some direct quotes from BOBS 3Q 2012 10Q about the favourable relationship with its trade partners. Emphasis is mine.

"We enter into agreements with beverage and food suppliers and for each product, we negotiate a monthly performance bonus which will depend on the product sales volume to our chains (including both own-operated and franchise operated). **The performance bonus can be paid monthly or in advance (which are estimated), depending on the agreement terms negotiated with each supplier.** *The performance bonus is recognized as a credit in our Consolidated Statements of Operations (under "Revenues from Trade Partners"). Such revenue is recorded when cash*

from vendors is received, since it is difficult to estimate the receivable amount and significant doubts about its collectability exists until the vendor agrees with the exact bonus amounts."

'The rise in the number of franchisees, from 774 on September 30, 2011 to 916 on September 30, 2012, together with the expansion of the multi-brand concept, has given the Company's management greater bargaining power with its suppliers. *Such increase of point sales did not derived an increase on Revenue from Trade Partners from 2011 to 2012, because the Company had agreements with new trade partners during 2011 and 2010 which originated bonus paid in advance. The bonus recorded during 2012 was from the regular business since no further advances were received during 2012."*

BOBS also has several exclusivity agreements including with Coca-Cola (KO).

"We participate in long-term exclusivity agreements with Coca-Cola, for its soft-drink products, Ambev, the biggest Brazilian brewery company, Farm Frites, the Argentinean producer of French fries, and Sadia, one of the biggest meat processors in Brazil, as well as with Novartis Nutrition for its Ovomaltine chocolate. These agreements are extensive from four to five years. The Coca-Cola agreement was amended in 2008 to extend the exclusivity period to April 2013."

"Amounts received from the Coca-Cola exclusivity agreements (see note 12) as well as amounts received from other suppliers linked to exclusivity agreements are

recorded as deferred income and are being recognized on a straight line basis over the term of such agreements or the related supply agreement. The Company accounts for other supplier exclusivity fees on a straight-line basis over the related supply agreement. The Coca-Cola agreement was amended in 2000 to extend the exclusivity period to 2008. Later amended and extended until April, 2013. **Performance bonuses may also include exclusivity agreements, which are normally paid in advance by suppliers."**

Due to its growing size and economies of scale BOBS has gained a competitive advantage over competitors by being able to receive "bonus payments" in advance from some of its suppliers. Its size and scale has enabled the company to sign these preferential and exclusive agreements, which have helped expand BOBS competitive position and moat in my opinion. Another reason I think BOBS has at least a minor moat is because it has been able to raise prices in recent years without losing sales which has helped to raise margins.

BOBS has had these preferential agreements in place for years, and hopefully will be able to continue them for years to come.

Due to BOBS growing store count, the agreements above, and the moat that I think it has, BOBS has been able to improve its sales, cut its costs, and improve margins in recent years. Numbers in below charts are taken from Morningstar or BOBS filings.

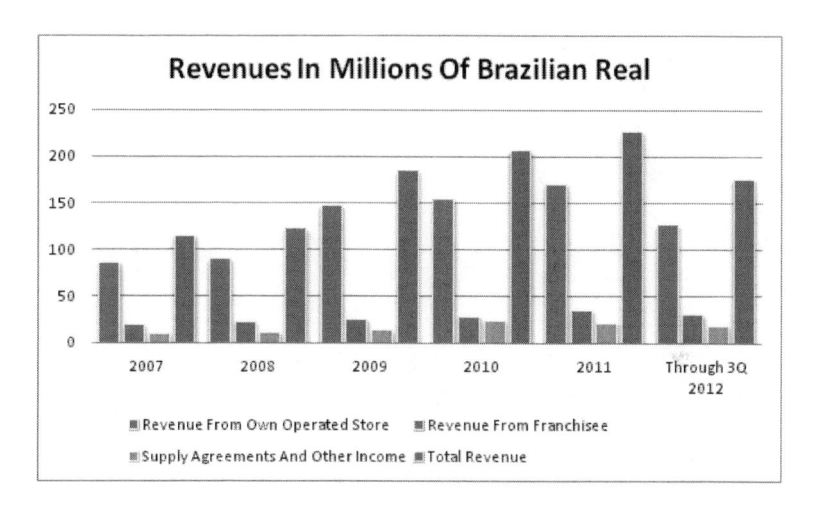

Revenues In Millions Of Brazilian Real

Year	Revenue From Own Operated Store	Revenue From Franchisee	Supply Agreements And Other Income	Total Revenue

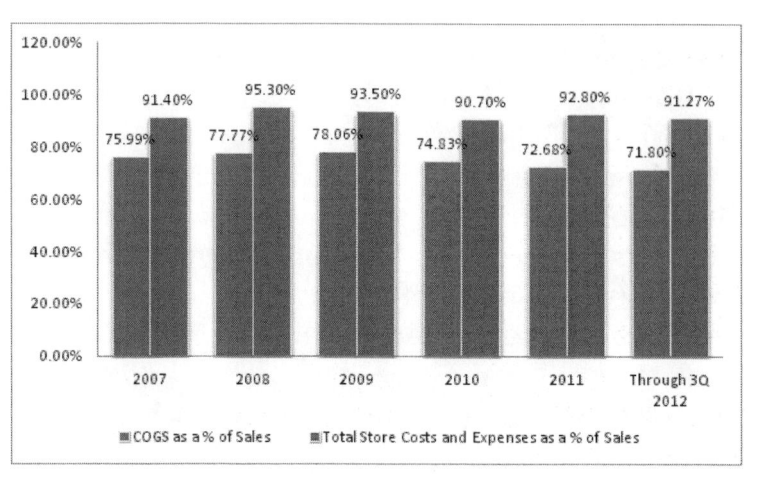

(Bar chart showing values for 2007, 2008, 2009, 2010, 2011, Through 3Q 2012)

COGS and Total Store Costs as % of Sales

Year	COGS as a % of Sales	Total Store Costs and Expenses as a % of Sales
2007	75.99%	91.40%
2008	77.77%	95.30%
2009	78.06%	93.50%
2010	74.83%	90.70%
2011	72.68%	92.80%
Through 3Q 2012	71.80%	91.27%

BOBS Margins

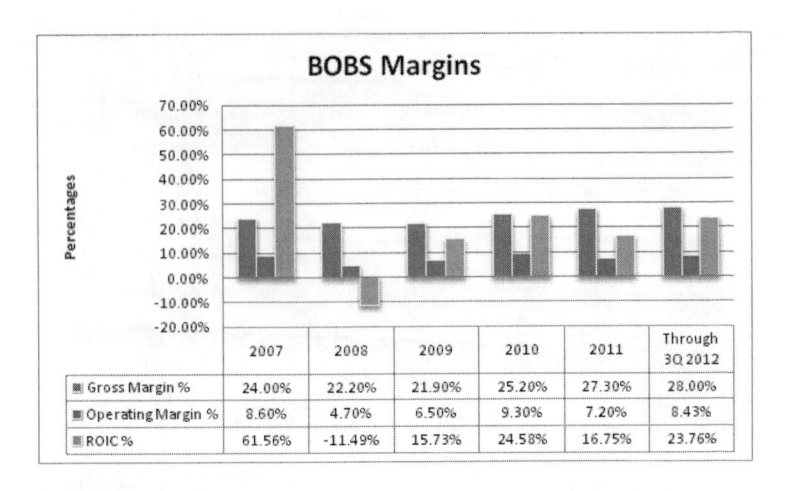

	2007	2008	2009	2010	2011	Through 3Q 2012
Gross Margin %	24.00%	22.20%	21.90%	25.20%	27.30%	28.00%
Operating Margin %	8.60%	4.70%	6.50%	9.30%	7.20%	8.43%
ROIC %	61.56%	-11.49%	15.73%	24.58%	16.75%	23.76%

As you can see in the above charts as BOBS restaurant count has grown, it sales have gone up, costs have gone down, and margins have gone up, substantially so since 2008. As BOBS continues to grow the same three things should continue to happen as BOBS should continue to compound its economies of scale: More restaurants means more sales, more restaurants means more compact grouping of restaurants which means lower costs and higher margins. It seems that BOBS has taken some lessons on how to cultivate and grow competitive advantages from companies such as Wal-Mart (WMT).

Margins

All numbers are taken from Morningstar, Yahoo Finance, or BOBS financial reports unless otherwise noted.

Gross Margin TTM	28.00%
Gross Margin 5 Year Average	24.12%
Gross Margin 10 Year Average	24.53%
Op Margin TTM	8.43%
Op Margin 5 Year Average	7.26%
Op Margin 10 Year Average	5.39%
ROE TTM	31.64%
ROE 5 Year Average	31.35%
ROIC TTM	23.76%
ROIC 5 Year Average	21.43%
My ROIC Calculation With Goodwill	45.10%

My ROIC Calculation Without Goodwill	48.30%
My ROIC TTM With Goodwill Using Total Obligations	15.56%
My ROIC TTM Without Goodwill Using Total Obligations	15.25%
FCF/Sales TTM	-3.54%
FCF/Sales 5 Year Average	-1.43%
FCF/Sales 10 Year Average	-1.39%
P/B Current	2.5
Insider Ownership Current	70.36%
My EV/EBIT Current	2.72
My TEV/EBIT Current	6.75
Working Capital TTM	22 $R

	Million
Working Capital 5 Yr Avg	0.4 $R Million
Working Capital 10 Yr Avg	-3.1 $R Million
Book Value Per Share Current	$3.17
Book Value Per Share 5 Yr Avg	$1.89
Float Score Current	0.88
Float Intensity	0.6
Debt Comparisons:	
Total Debt as a % of Balance Sheet TTM	16.78%
Total Debt as a % of Balance Sheet 5 year Average	16.40%

Current Assets to Current Liabilities	1.56
Total Debt to Equity	1.71
Total Debt to Total Assets	72%
Total Obligations and Debt/EBIT	4.36

Margin Thoughts

Please reference my Wendy's or Jack in the Box articles linked above to see how BOBS compares to the other fast food companies. TEV/EBIT and last three debt numbers talked about also include total obligations.

- Almost across the board BOB's margins have improved over the 5 and 10 year periods I looked at. Especially impressive are its ROE and ROIC.
- In comparison to the other fast food companies I have evaluated, BOBS margins are at worst about at the industry average or better than those companies margins.
- My estimates of ROIC make the company look absolutely exceptional as I estimate that without total obligations its ROIC is 45.1% with goodwill, and 48.3% without goodwill. Even if I count total obligations its ROIC with goodwill is 15.25%, and

without goodwill is 15.56%. Numbers that are close to McDonald's ROIC.
- Even if we just count BOBS 5 years average ROIC using Morningstar's numbers of 21.43%, which is what I used when I evaluated the other fast food companies, its margin is 6.35% points better than the industry average, and better than McDonald's by 4.05% points. Its ROIC is only bested by Yum Brands ROIC which is inflated by debt unlike BOBS.
- FCF/Sales for BOBS are worse than the industry average by 8.78% points and regularly negative over the past several years, and still negative this year.
- I think that its FCF/Sales margin is negative due to cap ex related to renovating and updating some of its restaurants.
- BOBS P/B is lower than the other fast food companies by a substantial margin. The only company with a lower P/B is Wendy's which as I talked about in my article on them, should be higher.
- Insider ownership above 70% for BOBS is fantastic, especially in comparison to the other fast food companies. BOBS is effectively a controlled family run company as four individuals own a combined 63.2% of BOBS as of the 2011 annual report: Ricardo Figueiredo Bomeny; the CEO and CFO of BOBS. Jose Ricardo Bosquet Bomeny; father of Ricardo and brother of Gustavo, business partner with Romulo and owns 20 of BOBS franchised restaurants. Romulo Borges Fonseca; owns 22 of

BOBS franchised restaurants and business partner with Jose. Gustavo Figueiredo Bomeny; brother of Jose and uncle of Ricardo.
- I am estimating BOBS EV/EBIT to be only 2.72 and it's TEV/EBIT to be only 6.75. BOBS EV/EBIT is lower than any company I have evaluated thus far and it is lower than the other fast food companies I have evaluated whose EV/EBIT average including Wendy's is 20.12. As I have stated before, I like to buy companies that have EV/EBIT and TEV/EBIT ratios lower than 8 so BOBS on a relative basis looks very cheap, especially when you consider it's very high ROE and ROIC and other margins that have grown.
- Book value has grown and BOB's debt levels look very sustainable to me.

Due to the sales and margin growth mentioned above, working capital has gone from negative for the better part of the past decade to now being solidly positive, BOB's accumulated deficit has almost disappeared, and shareholders equity has improved drastically, all of which can be seen in the chart below.

Numbers In Millions Of Brazilian Real

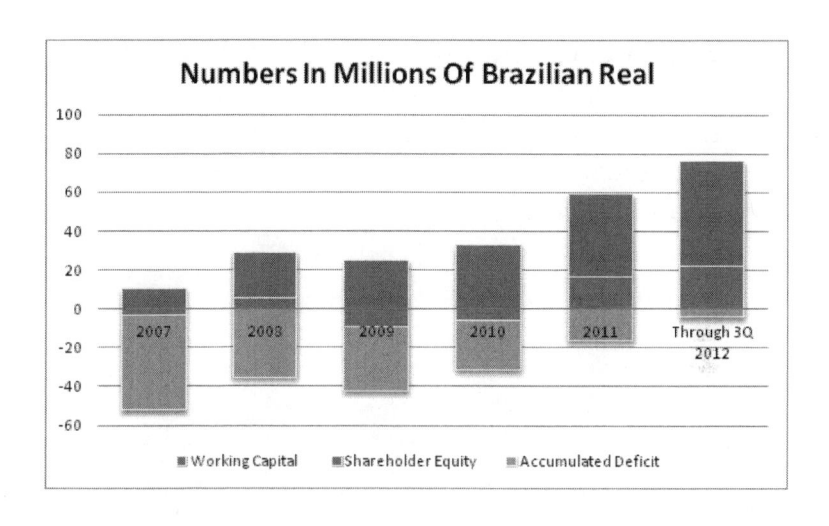

[Bar chart showing Working Capital, Shareholder Equity, and Accumulated Deficit from 2007 through 3Q 2012, with values ranging from approximately -60 to 80 million Brazilian Real]

Other Things of Note

- BOBS intends to focus its efforts on expanding both the number of its franchisees and the number of its franchised retail outlets, neither of which are expected to require significant capital expenditure. In addition, the expansion will provide income derived from initial franchise fees charged on new franchised locations.
- BOBS franchise agreements generally require the franchisee of a traditional Bob's burger restaurant to pay them an initial fee of $R 60,000, which is lower for kiosks and small stores, and additional monthly royalties fees equal to 5.0% of the franchisee's gross sales. Bob's fast food burger restaurants make up the vast majority of total restaurants in BOBS system.
- Lowered franchise fee in recent years from $R 90,000 to $R 60,000 to help attract more franchisees.

- BOBS has bought back shares recently and is authorized to buy back more shares. I think management has bought back shares at reasonable prices and I think now would be a good time to buy back even more shares. On December 5th, 2012 Mr. Romulo Borges Fonseca bought an additional 30,500 shares in the open market. I love to see buys from insiders who acquire their shares in the open market. Insiders generally only buy for a couple reasons: They think the company is undervalued, and/or that the company is going to perform well into the future.
- Operating margin for franchises used to be over 80%. Recently it has dropped into the mid 60% range and it seems to have stabilized in that area. It looks like the drop in franchise operating margin is due to franchise related costs rising.
- BOBS has been an OTC listed company for years, and this year it deregistered its shares with the SEC to save money every year, approximately $300,000. BOBS management says that it will continue to provide quarterly and annual reports to shareholders and that it will retain its reporting standards at the level they are at now. BOBS management has been in place for nearly 20 years so these things do not bother me that much as management has done a good job running the company over the years.
- Another reason BOBS deregistered its shares was because the company only had 51 current shareholders of its stock so the company is very

under followed and it probably was not worth it to register with the SEC.
- BOBS has substantial tax loss carry forwards NOL's: As of December 31, 2011 relating to income tax were R$31.6 million, $1.88 per share, and to social contribution tax were R$57.6 million, $3.42 per share. Social contribution tax is similar to the corporate tax here in the US.
- Due to its small size with a market cap around $65 million, only 51 shareholders, and it being a controlled company with 70% of BOBS owned by insiders and/or affiliates of the company, average daily volume is only 2,000 shares, and in the past two weeks about half of the days the market has been open there have been no shares traded.
- Same store sales have risen in the 4% range every year since 2007.

Intrinsic Valuations

Valuations were done using BOBS 2011 10K and 2012 third quarter 10Q. All numbers are in millions of Brazilian Real, except per share information, unless otherwise noted.

Low Estimate of Intrinsic Value

	Numbers:
Revenue:	237

Multiplied By:	
Average 5 year EBIT %:	7.26%
Equals:	
Estimated EBIT of:	16.99
Multiplied By:	
Assumed Fair Value Multiple of EBIT:	8X
Equals:	
Estimated Fair Enterprise Value of BOBS:	135.92
Plus:	
Cash, Cash Equivalents, and Short Term Investments:	28.4
Minus:	
Total Debt:	21
Equals:	
Estimated Fair Value of Common Equity:	143.32

Divided By: Number of Shares:	8.1
Equals:	17.69 R$ per share.
Equals:	$8.48 per share.

Base and High Estimate of Intrinsic Value

EBIT and net cash valuation

Cash and cash equivalents are 28.4

Short term investments are 0

Total current liabilities are 38.7

Number of shares are 8.1

Cash and cash equivalents + short-term investments - total current liabilities=

- 28.4-38.7=-10.3/8.1=-1.27 R$ per share=-$0.61 per in net cash per share.

BOBS has a trailing twelve month EBIT of.

5X, 8X, 11X, and 14X EBIT + cash and cash equivalents + short-term investments:

- 5X21.2=106+28.4=134.4/8.1=16.59 R$ per share=$7.93 per share.
- 8X21.2=169.6+28.4=198/8.1=24.44 R$ per share=$11.69 per share.
- 11X21.2=233.2+28.4=261.6/8.1=32.30 R$ per share=$15.45 per share.
- 14X21.2=296.8+28.4=325.2/8.1=40.15 R$ per share=$19.20 per share.

From this valuation I would use the 8X and 11X estimates of intrinsic value as my base and high estimates of intrinsic value respectively. None of the above valuations takes into account BOBS $5.30 per share worth of NOL's or BOBS future growth.

Relative Valuations

- As I said above, I like to buy companies whose EV/EBIT and TEV/EBIT ratios are lower than 8 and BOBS ratios are at 2.72 and 6.75 respectively. BOBS EV/EBIT ratio is the lowest I have found out of the companies that I have done full evaluations on.
- Its P/B ratio is also quite a bit lower than other fast food companies.

- BOBS P/E ratio of 9.1 is less than half of the industry P/E of 19.8.

I found BOBS to be cheap on an intrinsic value basis and it also looks to be equally cheap on a relative valuation basis. On an EV/EBIT basis, BOBS is the lowest valued company I have fully analyzed which is a bit shocking considering its high ROIC and other margins, and the moat that I think it has.

Competitors

- McDonald's (MCD): The number one fast food chain in Brazil and fast food behemoth around the world always provides stiff competition to smaller companies. Arcos Dorados (ARCO) is the largest operator of McDonald's restaurants in Latin America and the world's largest McDonald's franchisee. As of its 2011 10K it had 662 McDonald's restaurants in Brazil. Arcos Dorados' margins are quite a bit worse than BOBS margins and I would encourage you to read their annual reports for further information if you are interested in them or interested in comparing them to BOBS. Overall McDonald's has more than 1,000 restaurants in Brazil.
- Giraffas: A private company with around 400 restaurants most of which are in Brazil, it has recently started opening restaurants in South Florida. Serves similar food as Bob's burger chain.

- Yogoberry: Another private company who has more than 100 restaurants in Brazil. Will be competing with BOBS latest acquisition Yoggi's in the frozen yogurt and smoothie arena.
- Various other fast food offerings including from Japanese, Middle Eastern, and other typical fast food restaurants.

The fast food service industry is very competitive in Brazil as it is here in the US with peoples income being sought after by a plethora of restaurants and fast food companies. I think the major threat is of course McDonald's as BOBS other local competitors are generally quite a bit smaller than it. I think that due to the moat I see within BOBS, along with its growing size, and expansion into pizza, frozen yogurt, and chicken, that it can compete very well with the competition it has in Brazil and continue to grow its store count profitably.

Pros

- BOBS is cheap on an intrinsic value and relative value basis.
- I think BOBS has a small and growing moat that should continue to grow as BOBS restaurant count gets bigger.
- BOBS margins generally have grown over the past five years. In some cases by multiple percentage points. Some of BOBS margins are

even better than McDonald's and quite a bit better than Arcos Dorados' run McDonald's restaurants in Latin America.
- BOBS has signed exclusivity agreements with several companies including Coke, and also enjoys preferential agreements with its suppliers.
- BOBS has $5.30 per share worth of NOL's that are not even counted in any of my valuations.
- BOBS has a low and sustainable amount of debt.
- Its book value per share has grown.
- BOBS has almost eliminated its accumulated deficit, made its working capital positive after it being negative for most of the last decade, and substantially increased shareholders equity.
- COGS and total restaurants costs and expenses as percentages of sales have been lowered by multiple percentage points in recent years.
- The company is effectively controlled by four individuals who have thus far done a very good job of running the company.
- BOBS has bought back some shares while the company is undervalued and has the authorization to buy back more shares.
- BOBS can grow its restaurants through franchisees at minimal cap ex expenses. Franchise operating margin has been in the mid 60% range recently.
- Brazil has a growing middle class that should help grow sales further.

Cons

- Although I think BOBS has a small and growing moat, it may not be a long term sustainable competitive advantage due to competition and possible loss of exclusivity and preferential trade partner agreements.
- BOBS does not create consistent positive FCF.
- BOBS FCF/Sales margin is below the average of the other fast food companies I have evaluated and it is also negative.
- Franchise operating margin has dropped from over 80% to the mid 60% range in recent years.
- Stiff competition including McDonald's and now Burger King in Brazil.

Potential Catalysts

- Confederations Cup in 2013, FIFA World Cup in 2014, and the Olympics in 2016, all of which are in Brazil, will bring millions of tourists to Brazil which should help grow BOBS revenues further in the short and medium term.
- BOBS growing franchise store count will help grow BOBS moat as margins are very high and cap ex is very low when opening new franchised restaurants.
- BOBS moat may not be sustainable over the long term due to competition and possible loss of exclusivity and preferential trade partner agreements which would most likely hurt the company.

- Brazil's growing middle class should also help grow sales as more people come upon disposable income.

Conclusion

Brazil Fast Food Company, BOBS, has turned out to be a very interesting company to me. From its near death experiences in the mid 90's and early 2000's, to now being the number two fast food chain in Brazil, its growing store count and margins, and the various other things I have talked about in this article I have come away very impressed with BOBS as a whole and its management.

I think that BOBS is very undervalued on an intrinsic value and relative value basis and I think that it should conservatively be valued somewhere between $11.50 and $16.00 per share, not including the $5.30 per share in NOL's that it currently has.

Adding the NOL's to my estimates of value would take its estimated value up to between $16.50-$22 per share which is the range that I think BOBS should be selling at, and what I think its private market value is. Even leaving the NOL's out of the equation, BOBS is selling currently at only $8 per share which is a 32% discount to the absolute minimum I think BOBS is worth at $11.50 per share. I think that BOBS has a moat that could possibly grow over time, and that the company has catalysts in the short and medium term that could help unlock some of its value.

Warren Buffett always says that if you buy good companies that have some kind of moat at fair prices, that you will do very well investing over the years. I think BOBS is a good company with a moat that is currently selling at a very cheap price and I think I will do very well holding it over the years as I have bought its shares in my personal account and the accounts I manage.

Analysis Explanation

The chapters on Wendy's and BOBS were put back to back in this book intentionally so that you could contrast a poorly run, badly managed, barely profitable, growing but inefficient company, with a very well run, well-managed, very profitable, growing and very efficient company that are in the same industry. The two companies are polar opposites when it comes to evaluating each companies management and prospects as a potential investment and by this point in the book you should be able to decide which company was a better potential investment just by reading each company's annual reports, even if the companies names and stock tickers were blacked out.

There are three main differences between Wendy's and BOBS: Each companies cost/expenses and how that relates to their profitability, the lack of a moat at one and at least a small moat at the other, and the differences between how the two companies have been run over time by their respective managements.

Firstly is that while Wendy's costs and expenses have risen or stayed steady over the years as a percentage of the balance sheet, BOBS costs and expenses have generally been falling as a percentage of its balance sheet.

This is why BOBS margins have grown over the years while Wendy's margins have been stagnant or falling. The falling and rising of these two companies margins are why the two are going in very different directions as it pertains to debt levels as well. Because Wendy's margins are very low and either falling or stagnant in recent years, Wendy's has continually had to issue debt just to sustain its current level of operations. Due to BOBS increasing profitability in recent years it has been able to pay down its accumulated deficit almost completely, increase working capital and shareholders equity substantially, and has very little debt and total obligations compared to Wendy's.

The second part of this is that Wendy's has no moat and I believe BOBS to have at least a small moat. Due to Wendy's low profitability, apparent growth at any cost mindset, continuing to have to issue debt to keep operations as they are now, and the myriad other issues listed in the chapter on them, I do not believe Wendy's to have any kind of competitive advantage.

Because of its increasing size and restaurant count, BOBS has been able to sign some preferential and exclusive agreements with some of its suppliers, including Coca Cola. These agreements allow BOBS to get "bonus payments" up front before even selling the product. This means it gets to count the money earned from those transactions before doing any of the hard work. These preferential agreements have enabled BOBS to lower costs and increase profitability which has led to a gradual increase in its ROIC over the years. BOBS ROIC is even on par with McDonald's, the undisputed king in fast food around the world. As BOBS continues to grow its restaurant count it should be able to continue to grow its moat as well for reasons that were pointed out in the chapter.

The third part of this is far superior management at BOBS when compared to Wendy's. You can see BOBS superior management in just about every aspect of the company when compared to Wendy's: Superior margins and ratios, lowering of costs and expenses over time, much more efficient growth, the cultivation of a moat, and the many other issues that were talked about in the two chapters on these companies.

The two things that stand out to me here about the two companies management though is the lack of related party and unsavory transactions at BOBS when compared to Wendy's, and the very high insider ownership at BOBS.

Some people do not like high insider ownership in smaller companies because the insiders have complete control of the company and sometimes can lead to the insiders milking the company of its profits as you will see in a later chapter. If a company's management is this good at growing the company (BOBS was actually near death multiple times before they took over) I am all for management being able to control the entire company.

BOBS superior long-term management is why I am also comfortable with the company deregistering with the SEC as well. BOBS has been an OTC company for years but this year it decided to deregister with the SEC meaning that it would not be overseen by them anymore.

Normally this would be a gigantic red flag for me but due to the companies amazing management over the last 20 years and the high insider ownership at the company I do not think that its management would do anything nefarious that would cost the insiders who own around 70% of BOBS potentially tens of millions of dollars.

Even with BOBS extreme undervaluation, fantastic margins, and all the other great things that were talked about in the chapter above, I would not have bought into them after seeing that it deregistered from the SEC without its exceptional management. Once again if you cannot trust management then you should not buy into the company no matter how undervalued they are or how clean their balance sheet is as you will be asking for trouble by buying into a company with management that you do not trust.

New Terms and How to Calculate ROIC

I highly recommend reading the definitions of the following terms from somewhere like investopedia.com as the definitions are pretty detailed and not always as straight forward as they seem, especially for working capital.

Accumulated Deficit-The amount of net loss that is incurred in a given year when a business shows a negative balance in its retained earnings. This is obviously bad as it eats into a company's shareholders equity, meaning the company's shares are worth less due to these losses, and are caused by unprofitability. You can see how this affects a company with the above chart that shows that as BOBS has become more profitable it has turned its previously consistently negative accumulated deficit very positive. This has in turn substantially increased working capital and shareholders equity meaning that BOBS value has increased.

Working Capital=Current assets-current liabilities. Generally this number is supposed to be positive. If it gets too high though it means that the company may be retaining too much inventory. This is very bad and can mean that the company's products are not selling as they were expected to sell. This can lead to having to write down or write off the inventory which will cause losses. Working capital can sometimes be a good thing even when it is negative which can happen at companies like McDonald's, Amazon, and Wal-Mart. Sometimes when working capital is negative it means that the companies customers are paying up front for the items they are purchasing. This means that the companies are turning inventory rates so rapidly that the company is getting rid of the inventory before they even have to pay for it. This is obviously a very good thing and is usually found in gigantic well-known companies that we all use every day.

Net Operating Loss Carry forwards-These come when a company has more tax deductions or losses than it has in taxable income. These can be carried forward and applied to future years and can mean that a company may not have to pay taxes for many years if it accumulates enough of these NOL's as it can use these carry forwards to pay taxes after regaining its profitability. Usually NOL's are earned when a company has a bad year with negative income and profitability so these are not necessarily good things in and of themselves. But if a company has a few bad years and then turns themselves around and starts becoming profitable like BOBS did, then these NOL's can add substantial value to a company. I discount these NOL's sometimes by as much as 50% just for the sake of conservatism as they can sometimes take years and decades to use. The NOL's also expire after a certain amount of years and is another reason I discount them just to be safe. These can be an extremely valuable hidden asset within a company's filings as these NOL's are usually only talked about in a few lines within potentially hundreds of pages of information in a company's annual report so make sure to look out for mentions of tax loss carry forwards, NOL's, net operating loss carry forwards, and other related terms.

ROIC: There are many ways to calculate ROIC but below are the ways I calculate this very important number.

1. ROIC=EBIT/(Equity-goodwill+debt-cash) This is a more conservative estimate of ROIC as it subtracts a company's goodwill which can sometimes substantially inflate a company's ROIC. This is the ROIC estimate I use a lot more often because it is a much more conservative and because of my bias against goodwill.
2. ROIC=EBIT/(Equity+debt-cash) If you are not as biased against goodwill as I am this may be a good way to calculate ROIC. Beware though that if a company has a lot of goodwill that this calculation will leave the companies ROIC artificially inflated and will show the company to be over optimistically profitable.

In the debt portion of the calculation I now include a company's total obligations and commitments as well as normal short and long-term debt which you were shown how to calculate in the previous chapter. I do this to see how a company is truly operating and how much profitability it truly produces. If you do not add the total obligations you again will see an overly optimistic ROIC here because in my opinion you cannot get a true estimate of a company's profitability without including all of its debt, obligations, and commitments.

New Relative Valuations

All relative valuations are pretty much the same. You can either put the company or companies you are evaluating, against a benchmark like has been shown throughout the book with EV/EBIT and TEV/EBIT.

These relative valuations can also be put up against the industry average or other companies relative valuations so you can compare them to see who is relatively the most undervalued. You can also get an estimate of the companies intrinsic value by using relative valuations as well.

For example let us say a company is selling at a P/B of 1 with a share price of $10. If the industry average P/B is 1.5 or 2, and you expect the company to eventually sell for one of those two amounts, the share price of the company would rise to $15 and $20 respectively. I do not rely on relative valuations to get my estimates of intrinsic value and I only use the relative valuations to see how a company stacks up against its industry or other competitors.

You can also compare the other intrinsic valuations that have been shown in this book against each other as well. Comparing companies like this can be a good way to find other companies to research as well as it enables you to easily compare and see which companies are the most undervalued.

For example the contrast between JACK, WEN, and BOBS is staggering on almost every level from margins, profitability, debt, and relative and intrinsic valuations. I find this kind of information especially useful when you are fully invested and you find another company you think would be a good investment.

If you keep a database of information you can easily compare new companies to ones you already own to see which ones are the most undervalued, which ones may be the best investments, and if you need to dump a company you already own because you have found a newer better company to buy into.

Chapter 11: Unico American Corporation (UNAM) January 2013. Insurance Companies Different Terms, Techniques, and Valuations, Float, Levered ROA, Site Recommendations, Negative EV, EV/EBIT, and TEV/EBIT.

"If our premiums exceed the total of our expenses and eventual losses, we register an underwriting profit that adds to the investment income our float produces. When such a profit is earned, we enjoy the use of free money – and, better yet, get PAID for holding it. That's like your taking out a loan and having the bank pay YOU interest." Warren Buffett

Introduction and History

When starting to read about Unico American Corporation (UNAM) I was expecting to just use this as a learning experience since this is the first insurance company that I have truly evaluated. I was planning on learning the important insurance industry terms, what they meant, how they affected the company in question, what the float was and how that affected the company's operations, etc, and analyzing the company using all the knowledge I have gained lately from my recent foray into studying float and put those findings into an article. I was not expecting to find what I did: A company that is undervalued by EVERY ONE of my estimates of value, a company that has been for a number of years very disciplined and conservative in its estimates, which I found are of utmost importance in the property and casualty insurance business, and a company that has had underwriting profits every year since 2004, which I found out is really hard to do. If I had the capital available I would love to own this entire company and to build my investment firm with this company at the core, à la Warren Buffett with Berkshire Hathaway and its insurance companies. However, unless someone out there would like to endow me with nearly $100 million I will just have to be happy buying shares in UNAM and watching my money compound into the future.

UNAM is a relatively small (Current market cap around $65 million) holding company whose main subsidiary, Crusader, is a property and casualty insurance company who writes insurance only in the state of California. The vast majority of its operations (around 98%) are in commercial multi peril insurance writing. UNAM also has some other subsidiaries that operate in various insurance related industries, but for this article I am only going to concentrate on

Crusader and UNAM as a whole as its other subsidiaries contribute only fractionally to UNAM's results. UNAM used to write insurance in a number of other states but decided to concentrate only on California as it was generally losing money on its insurance operations in those other states. UNAM is still licensed to write insurance in several other states so it may choose to expand back into those areas but at this time it appears to be content expanding throughout California. The below quoted areas are from UNAM's annual reports about the previous business in other states and why its management decided to stop those operations.

"In 2002 the Company began to substantially reduce the offering of insurance outside of California primarily due to the unprofitability of that business.

In 2004 all business outside of California had ceased. In 2002, primarily as a result of losses from liquor and premises liability coverage which had rendered much of the Company's business outside of California unprofitable, the Company began placing moratoriums on non-California business on a state-by-state basis. By July 2003, the Company had placed moratoriums on all non-California business. The Company has no plan to expand into additional states or to expand its marketing channels. Instead, the company intends to allocate its resources toward improving its California business rates, rules, and forms.

The Company incurred underwriting losses in 2000, 2001, and 2002. As a result of these underwriting losses, management analyzed and acted upon various components of its underwriting activity. The Company believes that the implementation of these actions contributed to the improved underwriting results. This is reflected in the decrease in the Company's ratio of losses and loss adjustment expenses to net earned premium from 139% in 2001, to 98% in 2002, to 85% in 2003, and to 69% in 2004."

As you will see throughout the rest of this article, UNAM's operations have changed drastically for the better since those decisions were made.

Overview of Operations

Below are descriptions of UNAM's insurance business taken from its annual reports. Emphasis is mine.

The insurance company operation is conducted through Crusader. Crusader is a multiple line property and casualty insurance company that began transacting business on January 1, 1985. Since 2004, all Crusader business has been written in the state of California. During the year ended December 31, 2011, about 98% of Crusader's business was commercial multiple peril policies. Commercial multiple peril policies provide a combination of property and liability coverage for businesses. Commercial property coverage insures against loss or damage to buildings, inventory and equipment from natural disasters, including hurricanes, windstorms, hail, water, explosions, severe winter weather, and other events such as theft and vandalism, fires, storms, and financial loss due to business interruption resulting from covered property damage. **However, Crusader does not write earthquake coverage.** Commercial liability coverage insures against third-party liability from accidents occurring on the insured's premises or arising out of its operation. In addition to commercial multiple peril policies, Crusader also writes separate policies to insure commercial property and commercial liability risks on a mono-line basis. Crusader is domiciled in California; and as of December 31, 2011, Crusader was licensed as an admitted insurance carrier in the states of Arizona, California, Nevada, Oregon, and Washington.

The property casualty insurance marketplace continues to be intensely competitive as more and more insurers are competing for the same amount of customers. **Many of Crusader's competitors price their insurance at rates that the Company believes are inadequate to support an underwriting profit. While Crusader attempts to meet such competition with competitive prices, its emphasis is on service, promotion, and distribution. Crusader believes that rate adequacy is more important than premium growth and that underwriting profit (net earned premium less losses and loss adjustment expenses and policy acquisition costs) is its primary goal.** Nonetheless, Crusader believes that it can grow its sales and profitability by continuing to focus upon three areas of its operations: (1) product development, (2) improved service to retail brokers, and (3) appointment of captive and independent retail agents.

The property and casualty insurance industry, P&C insurance, has been in what is considered a "soft market" since 2004. A soft insurance market is characterized by rising costs, more competition, less profitability, and harder ability to make underwriting profits at all. UNAM has been disciplined enough during this soft insurance market of the past 8 years to achieve underwriting profits every year since 2004. As I will detail later that feat has been very hard to come by for other P&C insurance companies and is extremely impressive. The strict discipline to keep prices high enough to retain that underwriting profit has led to loss of business since 2004; net premiums written have dropped from $33 million in 2007 to just under $27 million in 2011. All numbers throughout this chapter are in millions $US unless otherwise noted.

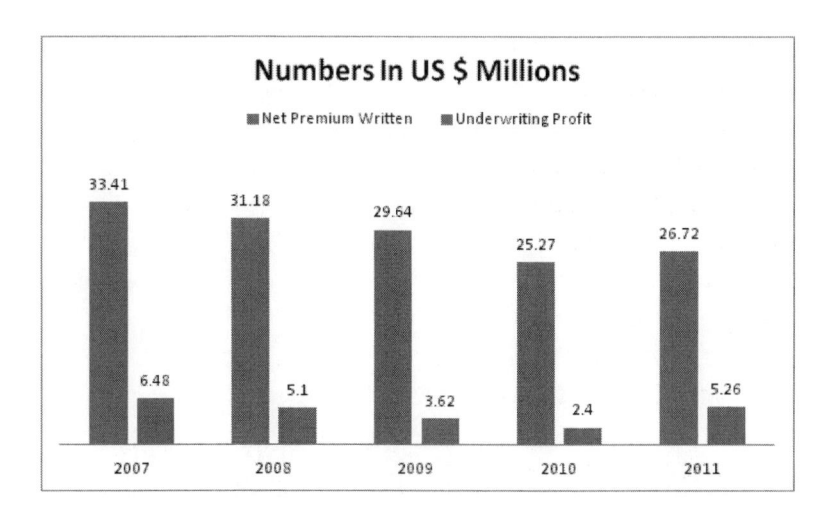

Numbers In US $ Millions

Year	Net Premium Written	Underwriting Profit
2007	33.41	6.48
2008	31.18	5.1
2009	29.64	3.62
2010	25.27	2.4
2011	26.72	5.26

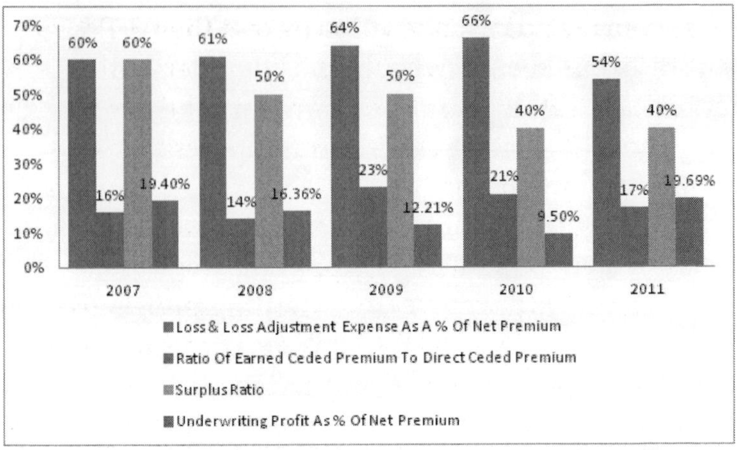
70%
60%
50%
40%
30%
20%
10%
0%
60%
16%
60%
19.40%
61%
14%
50%
16.36%
64%
23%
50%
12.21%
66%
21%
40%
9.50%
54%
17%
40%
19.69%
2007
2008
2009
2010
2011
Loss & Loss Adjustment Expense As A % Of Net Premium
Ratio Of Earned Ceded Premium To Direct Ceded Premium
Surplus Ratio
Underwriting Profit As % Of Net Premium

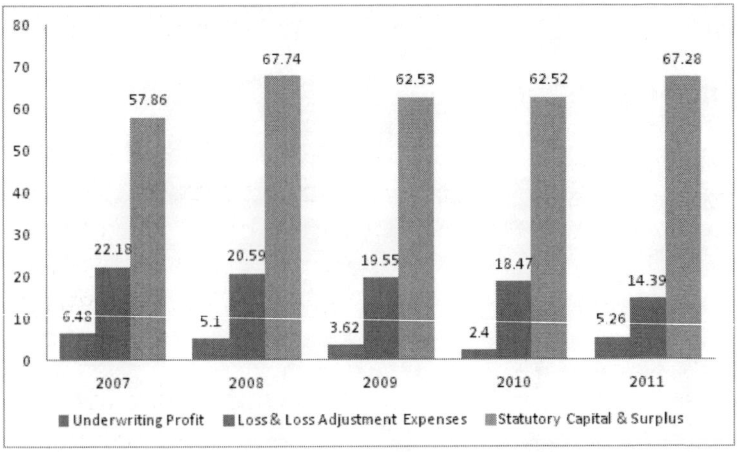
80
70
60
50
40
30
20
10
0
6.48
22.18
57.86
5.1
20.59
67.74
3.62
19.55
62.53
2.4
18.47
62.52
5.26
14.39
67.28
2007
2008
2009
2010
2011
Underwriting Profit
Loss & Loss Adjustment Expenses
Statutory Capital & Surplus

The surplus ratio is supposed to be less than 300% so UNAM is well underneath that. The underwriting profit as a % of net premium has consistently been between 9%-20% since 2007. Very impressive profit margins especially in comparison to some of the other insurance companies I researched and will talk about later that have underwriting losses. The statutory capital and surplus numbers is the amount of extra money after all liabilities and assets have been properly calculated according to the accounting standards. Generally the higher the better and the more money the company has to potentially invest and pay out claims with. Dividends can be paid out of the surplus capital as well.

I estimated what its profit numbers are for the whole of 2012 and I estimate an underwriting profit of 4.92, net premiums written of 33.21 and underwriting profit as a % of net premium of 14.81%. I did not include those in the above chart because those numbers are not official.

Last week I wrote about my conversation with Mr. Lester Aaron the CFO of the company and I posted my notes about that conversation on my blog that you can find by searching Unico. After thinking about it some more and after further research I am glad that UNAM has taken the attitude it has to be extremely disciplined and conservative in its investments as those decisions have generally paid off as I will show below.

After looking at some of its competitors I also noticed that P&C insurance companies generally invest 5% and less of their investment funds in equities to be sure that they have funds on hand in case of a catastrophic insurance event, so UNAM having no investments in equities does not seem to be as out of line with industry norms as I first thought. However, I think that UNAM should invest its $2 million self-imposed limit in equities to earn at least a somewhat better return than the about 1% it is earning now or at the very least get a bit more aggressive with buy backs and/or pay out more consistent special dividends with that money so that shareholders can put it to use. Earning 1% on investments is pretty much useless over the long-term so I hope management continues to do or starts doing some of the above things. In the past several years UNAM has occasionally paid out special dividends and bought back some of its shares.

Float Analysis

Unico American Corporation

- Financial Assets: Total investment 124.84+cash 0.09+accrued investment income 0.27+premium and notes receivable 6.02+unpaid loss and loss adjustment expense 7.81+defered policy acquisition costs 3.93+deferred income taxes 1.84=144.8
- Operating Assets: PP&E net 0.66+other assets 1.4=2.06
- Total Assets=146.86

Liabilities

- Equity of 75.23
- Debt of 0
- Float: Unpaid losses and loss adjustment expense 51.03+unearned premiums 16.6+advance premium and premium deposits 0.93+accrued expenses and other liabilities 3.1=71.66

Total liabilities are 71.66

Float/operating assets=71.66/2.06=34.79. Float is supporting operating assets almost 35X. Float is considered to be "free money" in this case because UNAM earns an underwriting profit and has since 2004.

Full year 2012 estimate of underwriting profit/total assets=ROA

- 4.92/146.86=3.37%

Full year estimate of underwriting profit/ (total assets-float) = levered ROA

- 4.92/75.2=6.54%

Competitors Info and Ratios and Comparison to UNAM

As I found out while researching other insurance companies to compare to UNAM, underwriting profit over a sustained period of years and the discipline to achieve that is very difficult. I looked at around 5-7 other insurance companies combined ratios and underwriting profits and found that only a couple of them had underwriting profits for more than two out of the last five years, and generally their combined ratios got much worse in the last three years. All of that makes UNAM's sustained underwriting profits since 2004 all the more impressive. Below are two of UNAM's competitors that I compared it to and their ratios.

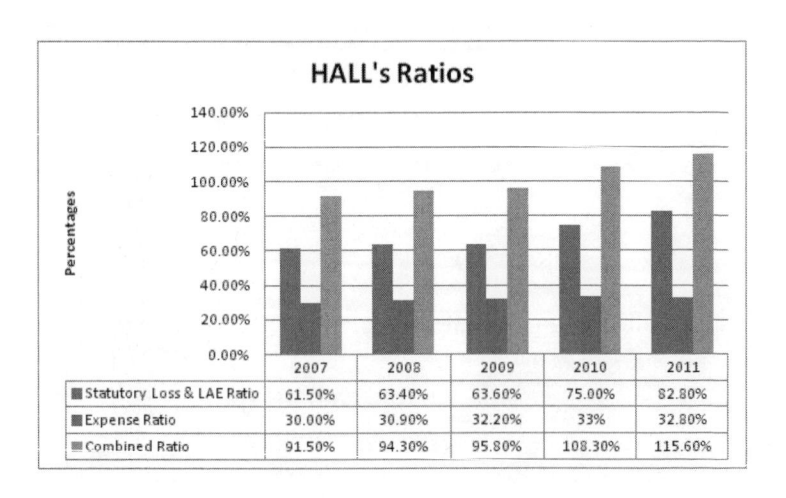

HALL's Ratios

	2007	2008	2009	2010	2011
Statutory Loss & LAE Ratio	61.50%	63.40%	63.60%	75.00%	82.80%
Expense Ratio	30.00%	30.90%	32.20%	33%	32.80%
Combined Ratio	91.50%	94.30%	95.80%	108.30%	115.60%

EIG's Ratios

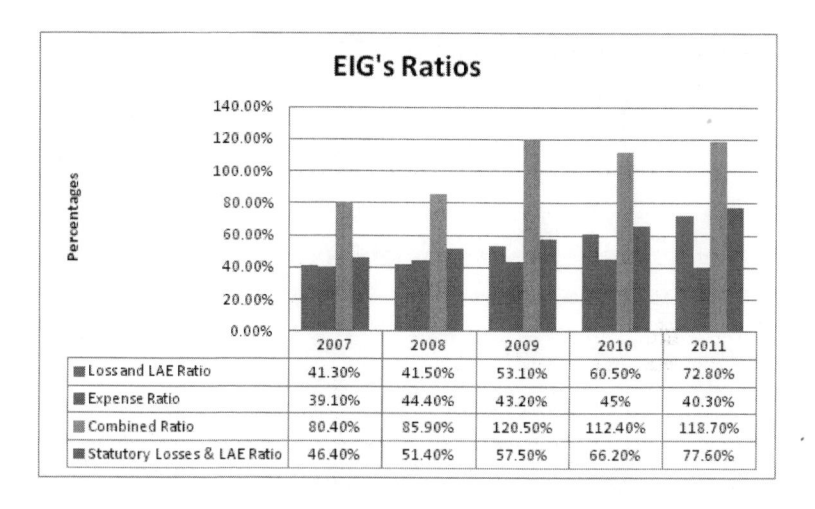

	2007	2008	2009	2010	2011
Loss and LAE Ratio	41.30%	41.50%	53.10%	60.50%	72.80%
Expense Ratio	39.10%	44.40%	43.20%	45%	40.30%
Combined Ratio	80.40%	85.90%	120.50%	112.40%	118.70%
Statutory Losses & LAE Ratio	46.40%	51.40%	57.50%	66.20%	77.60%

Of particular note is the giant leap in both companies Loss and LAE and combined ratios since 2007.

Those numbers are generally much worse than UNAM's ratios as you will see directly below.

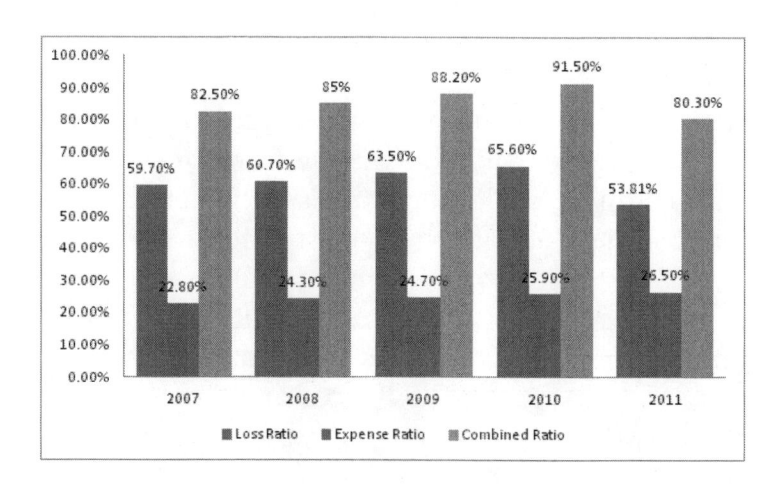

	2007	2008	2009	2010	2011
Loss Ratio	59.70%	60.70%	63.50%	65.60%	53.81%
Expense Ratio	22.80%	24.30%	24.70%	25.90%	26.50%
Combined Ratio	82.50%	85%	88.20%	91.50%	80.30%

UNAM's ratios have generally either stayed the same or gotten better since 2007. A drastic contrast to the other insurance companies I looked at, almost all of whose combined ratios have gotten worse since 2007.

Also of note is how the companies risk based capital ratio compares.

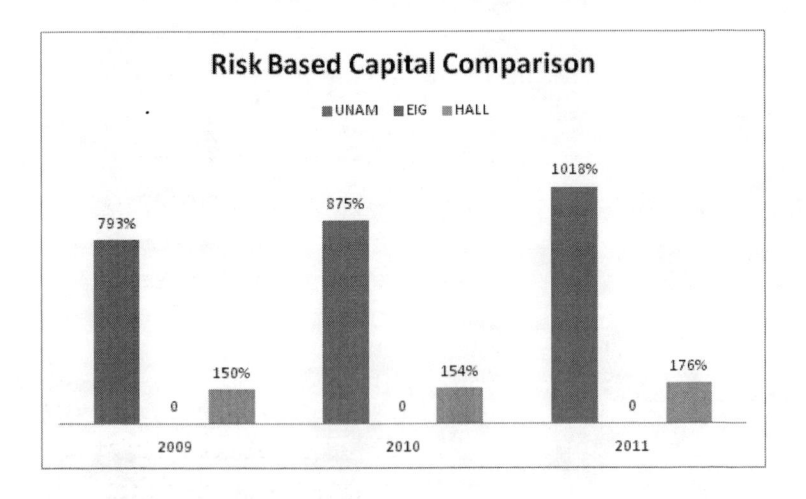

Risk Based Capital Comparison

UNAM ■ EIG ■ HALL

- 2009: UNAM 793%, EIG 0, HALL 150%
- 2010: UNAM 875%, EIG 0, HALL 154%
- 2011: UNAM 1018%, EIG 0, HALL 176%

The risk based capital numbers are supposed to be over 200% or insurance regulators may sanction or even take over the company as the company is deemed to be under potentially serious financial risk if its ratio is below 200%. Employer's Holding's (EIG) does not state what its RBC ratio is and only says that it exceeds the minimum requirement. I found that a lot of the other insurance companies I looked into also did not state what their RBC ratio was. As you can see Hallmark Financial (HALL) ratio has been under the minimum recommended 200% for a few years now.

I found out pretty quickly into my research that of paramount importance in the insurance industry is management discipline and conservatism. UNAM's management has shown an impressive amount of both and it has paid off as all the company's ratios have improved, sometimes substantially for the better as a lot of its competitors ratios are getting worse.

I found it very curious that pretty much all the insurance companies I looked at said that they were more primarily concerned with underwriting profits even if that meant that the number of premiums written declined. The reason I found that curious is because almost all of those other companies (outside of UNAM) had underwriting losses going back several years, sometimes while premiums written had grown.

So in some cases the other companies managements are at worst outright lying to its shareholders or at best being disingenuous with their stated underwriting policy as it relates to profitability. UNAM's managements focus, discipline, and conservatism appears to be an amazingly exceptional outlier in comparison to the other P&C insurance companies I looked at in terms of producing consistent underwriting profits.

Other Things of Note

- Generally there aren't any barriers of entry into the P&C insurance industry. The main advantage a company can gain is to be the low-cost operator,

but that sometimes comes with an underwriting loss as well.
- UNAM is a controlled company as Mr. Erwin Cheldin-former CEO, president, and chairman of the board of UNAM, Founder of UNAM, and father of Cary; Cary L. Cheldin-Chairman of the board, president, and CEO of UNAM, son of Erwin Cheldin; Lester A. Aaron-treasurer, director, and CFO of UNAM; and George C. Gilpatrick-director of UNAM, hold approximately 53.20% of the voting power of the Company and have agreed to vote the shares of common stock held by each of them so as to elect each of them to the Board of Directors and to vote on all other matters as they may agree.
- Biglari Capital, run by activist investor Sardar Biglari who tries to emulate Warren Buffett, owns 9.48% of UNAM. His fund has had recent discussions with UNAM. Nothing to report yet but Mr. Biglari has already tried to buy an insurance company before.
- Schwartz Value and Ave Marie Catholic Values combined own 8.51% of UNAM.
- Dimensional Fund Advisors owns 8.73% of UNAM.
- All of the above shareholders combine to own 79.92% of UNAM. Combine that with various other funds that own smaller portions of UNAM and probably fewer than 10%, less than 500,000 shares, of the company's shares are truly outstanding.

- Cary Cheldin and Lester Aaron, both of whom are executives of UNAM, are also on the company's compensation committee.
- On September 29, 2003, the Company borrowed $1,000,000 from Erwin Cheldin, director and the Company's principal shareholder, president and chief executive officer, and $500,000 from The Cary and Danielle Cheldin Family Trust. Very dedicated and committed shareholders and owners.
- Book value per share has risen. The nine-year average book value per share is $11.36 per share and currently UNAM's TTM book value per share is $14.12 per share. UNAM is currently selling for less than its book value per share.
- Revenues have dropped every year since 2004 when the soft insurance market started from a high of 62 down to a present TTM of 33.
- UNAM has a negative EV, TEV/EBIT, and EV/EBIT.
- UNAM's AM Best rating is A- which is deemed excellent. The AM Best rating is a measure of financial strength.
- UNAM has four reinsurers all of whom have AM Best ratings of A of higher.
- UNAM looks to be properly covered if a catastrophic insurance event happens as it carries a substantial amount of short-term investments, currently worth more than its entire current market cap. It also has substantial statutory capital and surplus, also currently worth more than its current market cap, and adequate reinsurance.

Valuations

Valuations were done using UNAM's 2011 10K and 2012 third quarter 10Q. All numbers are in millions of US$, except per share information, unless otherwise noted.

Absolute Minimum Valuation

This valuation is expecting 1% interest rates for the long-term and no growth in float over time.

- (Float X 10%) + Equity=estimated value/number of shares.
- (71.66 X 10%) +75.23=82.40/5.3=$15.55 per share.

Base Valuation

- Float + Equity=estimated value/number of shares.
- 71.66+75.23=146.89/5.3=$27.72 per share.

High Valuation

Assets:	Book Value:	Reproduction Value:
Fixed Maturity Securities	47	40
Short Term Investments	78	78
Premiums and Other Receivables	6	3
Deferred Policy Acquisition	4	2
Deferred Income Taxes	2	1
PP&E Net	1	0
Other Assets	9	4

Total Assets	147	128

Number of shares are 5.3

Reproduction Value

- 128/5.3=$24.15 per share.

This valuation does not take into account any of UNAM's float at all. Add float onto that asset reproduction value gets us to:

- 128+71.66=199.66/5.3=$37.67 per share.

Valuation Thoughts

- Current share price is $12.25 per share.
- UNAM appears to be massively undervalued. There is a 22% margin of safety to my absolute minimum estimate of intrinsic value. I actually think UNAM's true intrinsic value is somewhere in the $25-$35 range which would either be a double or triple from today's prices. These estimates of value do not even count the company's potential future growth in float, premiums, and investable money over time. My estimates of value also do not count on the insurance industry as a whole improving either, which will happen eventually.

- UNAM's downside is at least somewhat protected by its investments as well as it is currently selling for less than just the value of its short-term investments, which mostly consist of cash, cash equivalents, and CDs. Current per share value of short-term investment is $14.72 per share.
- I also found UNAM to be undervalued with every one of my other valuations.
- UNAM is selling for less than just what its float is worth per share at book value, $13.52 per share.
- UNAM is selling for less than the per share value of just its net assets after subtracting all liabilities including float, $14.15 per share.

Pros

- UNAM is undervalued by every one of my estimates of intrinsic value. As an example, UNAM's per share price is lower now than the per share value of JUST its short-term investments.
- UNAM's management looks to be very disciplined and conservative, which I found is of absolute importance in the insurance industry.
- Sardar Biglari, an activist investor, has recently bought just fewer than 10% of UNAM and may look to buy it outright as Mr. Biglari has already tried to buy an insurance company before. At the very least he could try to help unlock some of the value of UNAM's shares by working with management and has already had contact with UNAM management.

- UNAM has a negative enterprise value. There is an article on my blog from the site Greenbackd explains why that can be a good thing for shareholders as a negative enterprise value can mean a value dislocation.
- UNAM has earned an underwriting profit every year since 2004. More impressive is that 2004 started a soft market in the insurance industry which generally means it is harder to earn an underwriting profit.
- Even though UNAM is only earning 1% on its investments currently, UNAM still should have enough funds on hand to pay claims if a catastrophic insurance event happens as its surplus and statutory capital has grown substantially in recent years. UNAM actually has more in just statutory capital and surplus than its current total market cap. UNAM also has more in short-term investments than its current entire market cap and it also looks to be adequately reinsured.
- Book value per share has risen in recent years.
- UNAM's management seems to be dedicated to the company as the current CEO and his wife loaned the company money in 2003 when it was having some problems.
- Although UNAM's CEO and CFO are on its compensation committee, their pay seems fair to me.
- The former CEO, former president and founder, current CEO and president, and CFO own substantial portions of UNAM.

- In recent years UNAM has bought back some of its shares and paid special dividends on occasion because "We think that the shareholders can put the dividends to better use than I think that we can currently in the market." Quote from my conversation with the companies CFO Mr. Lester Aaron. That comment is very shareholder friendly.
- My entire conversation that I had with Mr. Aaron that you can find on my blog gave me confidence in management and laid some of my concerns to rest.
- All of UNAM's risk and insurance industry related ratios are far in excess of what they need to be and far better than its competitors that I looked at.
- UNAM's float should be considered as free money and looked at as kind of a revolving fund since it earns, and has earned since 2004, underwriting profits.
- UNAM has no debt. Some of the other insurance companies I looked at had to take on debt just to keep their operations out of regulators hands in recent years.

Cons

- Revenue and premiums written have generally dropped every year since 2004.
- UNAM is currently only earning 1% on its investments. This could mean that if a catastrophic insurance event happens in the

future that UNAM may not have enough money to pay claims.
- UNAM may be too conservative with the investments it owns and the company seems to have a lot of excess capital not being utilized at all currently.
- The current CEO and CFO are on UNAM's compensation committee.
- Some would say that UNAM's special dividends in recent years are just being paid to further pay the insiders of the company who own large portions of the company.

Catalysts

- Mr. Biglari could try to influence UNAM's management to help unlock some of the value of its shares, or buy the company outright as Mr. Biglari has already tried to buy an insurance company before.
- An improvement in the overall insurance industry could help unlock the value of UNAM.
- A catastrophic insurance event in California would harm UNAM's results.

Conclusion

This experience of learning about float over the last month or so has been an amazingly rewarding experience. As a relatively new investor I am always looking for opportunities to learn new things and expand my circle of competence and I think that I will look back years from now and see that this time period of my value investing journey was a turning point in getting me closer to my ultimate goals of opening up my own investment firm. As icing on the cake I also ended up finding another company to invest in as UNAM is a company that is undervalued by every one of my estimates of intrinsic value, has potential catalysts in place to help unlock value, has had underwriting profits since 2004, and has very focused, disciplined, and conservative management. For all the reasons I list above, UNAM is a company that I would like to own all of and build my investment firm around.

Update as I was getting ready to publish the article.

After I finished up writing the article at the end of last week I started reading The Davis Dynasty and realized I had a lot more I needed to learn about the insurance industry as a whole before being comfortable enough with my knowledge to make the decision to buy into UNAM. At this point I do not think that I have enough overall insurance industry knowledge to be able to make a definitive buy or sell decision so for now I am going to continue to learn about the insurance industry and when I feel I have enough knowledge, at that point I will make a definitive buy or sell decision about UNAM.

Hopefully UNAM's shares do not pop before I gain more knowledge as they are by far the best insurance company I have found up to this point but I do not want to repeat some of the mistakes I made in the past and buy something before I fully understand the business and industry it is in.

Analysis Explanation

I had heard about float especially as it pertains to insurance companies by reading a lot of stuff on Warren Buffett over the years and with the above article finally wanted to fully grasp the concept of float and how it can affect a company and greatly increase the value of said company. For about a month straight I took time off from the normal researching of companies and concentrated fully on learning about float, how it affects a company, where it can be found outside of the insurance industry, what makes float, and if a company has a good amount of float that usually means that it has at least a small moat. This learning endeavor culminated by analyzing a bunch of insurance companies and writing this article about UNAM. From my earlier minimal readings about float I understood that it was at least a mildly important factor in making Warren Buffett one of the best investors of all time. After my in-depth dig into understanding how it works the concept of float and coming to understand it fully is going to be one of the greatest lessons learned about evaluating companies and that it helped a great deal with Warren Buffett becoming who he is.

The power of float is extraordinary and to fully grasp it you should read all the best free materials I found online about it by searching my blog with the word float, Fundoo Professor, and Brooklyn Investor where all the most insightful links I found about float are shared. I also highly recommend reading The Davis Dynasty if you are interested in learning about the insurance industry and an amazing family of three generations of great investors as of the time the book was written. If there was one concept outside of learning the basics of how to value and analyze a company and developing your own investment processes, understanding float would be the other main thing that I recommend every serious value investor to learn about.

It needs to be illustrated here that you need to understand an industry very well before you should commit real money to buying into any company. After reading The Davis Dynasty I realized that I did not know nearly as much as I should about the insurance industry in general to be comfortable buying into UNAM so even though I thought it was a fantastic company that was substantially undervalued decided to pass on buying into the company at that time. The reason for this is twofold: If you do not understand the industry of the company you are buying into how can you evaluate whether it is a good buy or if it is undervalued sufficiently?

If you do not understand something reasonably well you are bound to make more mistakes than buying into something that you do understand well. This harkens back to Warren Buffett's concept of staying within your circle of competence and investing in things you understand so you make fewer mistakes. For example I generally do not even do research into financials other than insurance companies, mining/natural resource companies, or pharmaceuticals because I do not understand how they work, how to analyze them, or how to value them. Buying into a mining company when first learning about investing was actually one of my bigger early investment mistakes. I bought into Taseko Mines (TGB) because of the huge gold reserves and deposits they had at an undeveloped mining property that they owned. Come to find out later after actually doing the research that should have been done before that, that the mine was undeveloped because of concerns by Native Americans in Canada because the mine is located on land that is owned by the Native Americans. Taseko has fought with local and federal governments in Canada for years to start developing the mine to no avail and as of the time of the writing of this book the property is still not being developed.

If you do all the work, think it's a good company that is undervalued, but you feel that you still do not understand the industry enough then walk away for the time being and come back later after you have learned more about the company and industry. Doing this will save you a lot of money and frustrations and is something I wish I would have done a lot earlier in my investing journey.

New Terms

Negative Enterprise value, total enterprise value, EV/EBIT, and TEV/EBIT- You can find a great discussion of negative enterprise value by searching for Greenbackd on my blog where he explains why some of the companies that have negative enterprise values can be very good investments. A company with a negative enterprise value could mean that there is a value dislocation within a company's stock which means that a company could be undervalued, sometimes substantially.

Negative EV and TEV come about when a company has more cash, cash equivalents, and short-term investments than the company's equity and debt are worth. This can obviously be a very good thing especially if you are as very conservative value investor.

Before moving on to the next chapter I want to also illustrate the work it takes to become an excellent value investor and again how this book and connecting blog can help cut that time commitment down substantially. When starting to learn about float I only had a very basic understanding of the concept so when the learning started I was starting with an almost completely clean slate. It took me a month plus, probably a few hundred hours in total, of digging through the internet to find the best information about float. Wanting to get better like this takes a lot of dedication and willpower but it is necessary if you want to become an excellent value investor. The quicker you learn more concepts and techniques the less time requirement that will be required later and then you can concentrate on practicing what you have been learning. Learning compounds like money does. Best of all is that as has been outlined in this book most of the information I have learned from can be found either by reading and studying this book and searching my blog. I have listed all the very best information on my blog for easy access to all the best pages, books, articles, videos, etc that I learned from to help save you the years of time it took me to find all of this information.

The next three chapters will be showing you how to compare two or more companies in different industries with each other to determine which one is a better buy and if any of the companies you evaluated are worthy of buying into.

Chapter 12: Bab Inc (BABB) March 2013. Incorporating NOL's Into Valuations, Relative Valuations, Excessive Payroll, Customer Reviews, Overpriced Products, and Management.

"There is an enormous number of managers who have retired on the job." Peter Drucker

Introduction and Overview

The company I will be talking about in this article is BAB Systems Inc, (BABB) a very small and unfollowed $4.4 million market cap that is traded on the OTC market, company based in Deerfield, Illinois which is the parent company and franchise owner of My Favorite Muffin, Sweet Duet Frozen Yogurt & Gourmet Muffins, and Big Apple Bagels stores. BABB also sells Brewster's Coffee at its restaurants. As of August 31, 2012 BABB had 97 franchise units and 6 licensed units in operation in 24 states and zero owned stores after selling the only one last year.

BABB's revenues are derived primarily from the ongoing royalties paid to it by its franchisees and from receipt of initial franchise fees. BABB also gets income from the sale of its trademark bagels, muffins and coffee through nontraditional channels of distribution including to Mrs. Fields Famous Brands (Mrs. Fields), Kohr Bros. Frozen Custard, Braeda Cafe, Kaleidoscoops, Green Beans Coffee, Sodexo and through direct home delivery of specialty muffin gift baskets and coffee. Below are descriptions of the different operating segments taken from BABB's annual and quarterly reports.

Big Apple Bagels

BAB franchised stores daily bake a variety of fresh bagels and offer up to 11 varieties of cream cheese spreads. Stores also offer a variety of breakfast and lunch bagel sandwiches, salads, soups, various dessert items, fruit smoothies, gourmet coffees and other beverages.

My Favorite Muffin

MFM franchised stores daily bake 20 to 25 varieties of muffins from over 250 recipes, plus a variety of bagels. They also serve gourmet coffees, beverages and, at My Favorite Muffin and Bagel Cafe locations, a variety of bagel sandwiches and related products.

Brewster's Coffee

Although the Company doesn't have, or actively market, Brewster's stand-alone franchises, Brewster's coffee products are sold in most of the franchised units.

Sweet Duet Frozen Yogurt

On May 7, 2012 the Company issued a press release announcing the launch of its new franchise concept SweetDuet Frozen Yogurt & Gourmet Muffins, which it is preparing to roll out this year. While BAB will be offering franchises in all 50 states, its initial development focus is targeted for the Midwest, specifically Illinois, Michigan, Wisconsin and Ohio. As part of its introductory development plan, BAB will be donating 10% of the initial franchise fee from its first 50 units to the Cystic Fibrosis Foundation, of which BAB is a corporate sponsor. SweetDuet, as its name implies, is a fusion concept, pairing self-serve frozen yogurt with BAB's exclusive line of My Favorite Muffin gourmet muffins, broadening the shop's offering and therefore differentiating itself from the numerous frozen yogurt outlets already populating the market. SweetDuet Frozen Yogurt & Gourmet Muffins shops will also include BAB's. Brewster's Coffee and a streamlined breakfast menu. The concept is designed to work in 1600 square feet of space. The SweetDuet concept will be included as part of the Systems franchise operating and financial information.

Typically these restaurants seat around 30 people.

Operations and Management Discussion

Currently BABB's is pretty much a holding company operation now that it does not directly run any of its restaurants and it derives its revenue from collecting royalty fees from its franchisees (5% of net sales.) Initial franchise fees when a new store opens ($25,000 for a franchisees first "Full production" Big Apple Bagels or My Favorite Muffin. Fee for subsequent stores opened by franchisees is $20,000.) Big Apple Bagel and My Favorite Muffin franchisees also contribute 3% of net sales towards advertising and marketing to BABB.

Since BABB does not directly operate any restaurants, and it just does corporate back office work for the whole company, locates new franchisees and franchise locations, markets the company, and sits back to collect fees from the franchisees of course you would expect BABB to have absolutely exceptional margins.

The company does have some pretty good TTM margins: Gross margin at 96.2%, operating margin at 17.9%, ROE of 15.51%, and an ROIC of 14.51%. However the companies operating margin, ROE, and ROIC could potentially double if payroll and payroll related expenses could be halved from their extremely high current levels (Which is probably a bit optimistic and I will talk about more below) and didn't amount to more than $1 million, or about 25% of the companies entire market cap, and about 1/3 of its enterprise value.

If payroll and payroll related expenses which totaled about $1.4 million for the entirety of 2011, or 53% of BABB's gross profit, (An incredible $100,000 per employee at a $4.4 million market cap company) could be cut in half that would add 9 cents to BABB's EPS, which would almost triple current EPS. Cutting payroll expenses by half is just an estimate of what the company could do and may be a bit optimistic but BABB management should certainly be able to get close to halving payroll if it really wanted to become a more efficient company. That 9 cents per share extra could be put towards growing the company further, paying an even bigger dividend (current dividend yield is 3.31%), or my favorite option, buying back shares outstanding since I am finding BABB to be undervalued currently and which I will talk about later. Just the top three executives of the company made nearly $700,000 in 2011, not including the also generous options that have been given in the past, are still being given, and can still be exercised for even higher compensation for the three main executives of BABB. Company insiders do own about 38% of BABB but that is down from a few years ago where insiders owned 48% of BABB.

At November 30, 2011 there are 360,400 of unexercised options that are not included in the computation of dilutive EPS because their impact would be antidilutive due to the market price of the common stock being higher than the option prices. At November 30, 2010 there were 368,373 unexercised options that were not included in diluted EPS because their impact would be antidilutive due to the market price of the common stock being higher than the option prices.

Executive pay has also been rising in most recent years even as the number of total restaurants franchised and owned has dropped from 129 total restaurants in 2007 down to 103 total restaurants. Since BABB no longer operates any of its restaurants the drop in number of total restaurants has also dropped royalty income, operating income and total company value. Again, executive pay has continued to rise in recent years as this has been going on.

On top of all of this the CEO Mr. Michael G. Evans, is on BABB's compensation committee which never looks good, especially in this case due to the high executive pay in comparison to the overall size of the company.

Also of note as it pertains to how the company operates is that as I talked about above the company receives 3% of net sales towards marketing and advertising for the restaurants. This amount for several years now at year-end has stayed consistently in the $300,000 a year range in unused advertising and marketing funds that the company could be putting towards better use than just sitting in company accounts waiting to be used.

Management could also be getting a bit sidetracked with opening up its new restaurant concept Sweetduet Frozen Yogurt as well and may be better served concentrating on and improving its already established Big Apple Bagel and My Favorite Muffin restaurants.

Valuations

This section will illustrate why I think management could be doing a much better job, especially when it comes to their own pay, and putting some of that money to better use for shareholders.

Valuations were done using BABB's 2011 10K and 2012 third quarter 10Q. All numbers are in thousands of US$, except per share information, unless otherwise noted.

Cash and NOL Valuation (Absolute Minimum Valuation)

- BABB has 1,239 in cash (17 cents per share) + total net operating loss carry forwards of $5,857, discounted 50% which I will talk about later to $2,928 (40 cents a share)= a total valuation of 57 cents per share.

EBIT, Cash, and NOL Valuation

Cash, cash equivalents, and short-term investments are 1,239

Total current liabilities are 822

Number of shares are 7,266

Cash and cash equivalents + short-term investments - total current liabilities=

- 1239-822=417/7266=$0.06 in net cash per share.

BABB has a trailing twelve month EBIT of 504.

5X, 8X, 11X, and 14X EBIT + cash and cash equivalents + short-term investments+$2,928 in NOL's, or $0.40 per share:

- 5X504=2520+1239=3759/7266=$0.52 per share+$0.40 in NOL's=$0.92 per share.

- 8X504=4032+1239=5271/7266=$0.73 per share+$0.40 in NOL's=$1.13 per share.
- 11X504=5544+1239=6783/7266=$0.93 per share+$0.40 in NOL's=$1.33 per share.
- 14X504=7056+1239=8295/7266=$1.14 per share+$0.40 in NOL's=$1.54 per share.

Right now BABB's operations at 5X EBIT are only adding 2,520 (35 cents per share) to its overall valuation due to overall restaurant count dropping and now only collecting royalty, license, and franchise fees but even at that valuation BABB is selling at a 35% discount to today's share price of 60 cents a share. I chose to discount the NOL's by 50% in the above valuations for conservatism because a lot of these NOL's will take years to accrue to BABB.

Relative Valuations

- BABB's P/E is currently 9 with the industry average being 17.9. With BABB's current share price of 60 cents per share, if it was selling at the industry average P/E it would be worth $1.20 per share.
- BABB's P/B is currently 1.4 with the industry average being 3.7. With BABB's current share price of 60 cents per share, if it was selling at the industry average P/B it would be worth $1.58 per share.
- BABB's TEV/EBIT is 7.07 and its EV/EBIT is 6.58. Both of which are under 8 which is

generally what I like to see in companies I think about buying into.

Valuation Thoughts

- BABB's, which is currently selling at 60 cents per share, is undervalued by every one of my estimates of intrinsic and relative value estimates when compared to its industry.
- BABB has $153,000 in total debt, or only 2 cents per share so even subtracting the company's debt it is still undervalued.
- By my absolute minimum estimate of value BABB is valued about fairly right now but that only includes cash and NOL's. Adding in BABB's operations into the valuation makes BABB undervalued by 35% currently.

Customer Reviews

As I have researched and wrote this article one thing has continued to bother me and not made very much sense about BABB. The restaurant count dropping has been a bit perplexing to me as the company has been profitable every year since 2002 except for 2009, and I would not have thought that bagel sales would have suffered a massive drop during the recession, so the restaurant count dropping in 2007 from 129 total restaurants to now only having 103 total restaurants (Or a reduction in total restaurant count of 20%) has continued to bug me as the process of researching this company has gone on.

I have not eaten at any of BABB's restaurants before as the closest one of its restaurants are a six-hour drive away from me so I decided to find customer reviews online to help me get a bit of perspective on how the franchise restaurants are generally thought of by its customers.

After reading through dozens of customer reviews from different franchise locations I think that I am able to come to some conclusions about what its customers think about Big Apple Bagel restaurants and think that I have found the answer to the dropping restaurant count problem that has bothered me.

- Generally customers only think that the food is average to good.
- Generally people think that the bagel/sandwich products are overpriced.
- A lot of people thought that competitors have better bagels in their respective local areas.
- More than a few people mentioned that they only went to a BABB restaurant because of coupon promotions (buy 1 get 1 half off or free on bagel sandwiches.)
- More than a few people who said they went there only because of the coupons said that even with the coupon they thought the products were overpriced.
- The biggest overall concern that I saw stated over and over from customer visits to multiple different franchise locations was that customer service was rated at best ok to absolutely horrible.

Through my studies of many different companies in many different industries over the years I have learned many things that can help and hurt a company's sales and profitability. One of the biggest things that can help or hurt a company, especially in today's world where people can write things like customer reviews on the internet for everyone to see, is customer service or the lack thereof. I think that one of the reasons Amazon has been such a huge success is due to its customer service which is exceptional and one of the best I have ever dealt with. The reverse can also happen if you have a reputation for poor customer service and can lead to customers not coming back to your stores and restaurants.

Combine the poor customer service with products that the customers think are overpriced (even with buy 1 get 1 free coupons) and the combination of these two things may be why restaurant count has dropped by 20% in recent years. Maybe the restaurants are losing customers and sales, and the franchise locations are becoming unprofitable leading the franchisees to close restaurants. There is not really a mention of why the restaurant count has dropped in BABB's annual reports and to this point I have not been able to talk with company IR and have not had my phone calls returned to get these questions answered so for now this is my best guess as to why the number of restaurants have dropped in recent years.

Catalysts

- If management decided to cut payroll expenses and put that money towards much better use the share price would no doubt rise.
- Gaining more franchisees would up sales and profitability which would make the share price rise.

Pros

- BABB is at minimum fairly valued, and undervalued sometimes substantially with my other intrinsic and relative valuations.
- BABB's margins are pretty good overall.
- Insiders own around 38% of BABB.
- If BABB's management decided to cut payroll expenses it would raise EPS and overall profitability of BABB, potentially substantially depending on how much they decided to cut payroll.

Cons

- BABB's restaurant count has dropped by 20% since 2007 which has lowered the amount of royalty fees collected, thus lowering sales and profitability for the overall company.
- Management's pay is excessive in my view, taking up 53% of gross margin. Last year overall payroll and payroll expenses amounted to $1.4 million dollars with the company only having a

$4.4 million market cap. Stated another way payroll and payroll expenses make up 32% of the companies entire market cap.
- Just the top three executives of BABB made around $700,000 last year, not including options, or 16% of the entire market cap.
- BABB's margins could be a lot higher if management cut payroll expenses.
- A few years ago insiders owned 48% of the company and now only own 38%.
- At the very least the company is perceived to not have very good customer service, at worst BABB is viewed to have horrible customer service at some of its restaurants.
- Several reviewers online also thought the products sold at BABB restaurants were overpriced, even when they had a buy 1 get 1 half off or free coupon.

Conclusion

I will save in-depth talk about margins, float, and the other normal things I talk about in my articles for the conclusion piece in the series of posts but my overall investment thesis is very simple with this company: BABB is at worst fairly valued when only counting cash and NOL's and is undervalued by a substantial margin (about 35%) when including its operations.

If management were to cut payroll and other payroll expenses, especially executive pay and options, and put that money (Potentially as much as 9 cents per share if they were to halve payroll expenses) towards improving company operations and/or expanding the number of franchises, paying a higher dividend, or buying back shares, the company could potentially appreciate by even more.

In my opinion management could be doing a much better job helping this company expand and to improve operations, especially the customer service side of things. I do not think that BABB is necessarily a buy and hold forever company like some of the other companies I own, but I do think that BABB could grow its restaurant count, become more profitable, and turn into a much more attractive company to own, and potentially turn into a buyout candidate. Payroll expenses taking up 53% of gross profit is absolutely insane, and if BABB decides to cut some corporate excess/waste and put that money to much better use for shareholders and the overall company, BABB could potentially double or triple from today's current share price of 60 cents per share.

I still have a few more companies to write articles about before making a definite buy decision or not about BABB, but overall it looks like a potential investment opportunity at this point, especially if management would cut payroll expenses and put that money towards much better use for shareholders.

The next chapter will be about Paradise Fruit Company Inc (PARF) and we will save the explanations on both companies for the conclusion of the chapters about BABB and PARF.

Chapter 13: Paradise Inc (PARF.OB) March 2013. Finding The Value of Land, Property, and Equipment, Hidden Assets, Small Niches, Cash Conversion Cycle, Moats, and Relative Valuations.

"Value investing requires a great deal of hard work, unusually strict discipline, and a long-term investment horizon. Few are willing and able to devote sufficient time and effort to become value investors, and only a fraction of those have the proper mind-set to succeed." Seth Klarman

Introduction, History, Management Discussion, and Overview of Operations

Paradise began as a subsidiary of a different diversified corporation soon after World War 2, but very soon afterward candied fruit became the focus of its business. Current ownership purchased the company in 1961 and the name Paradise Fruit Company was adopted in 1965. It later changed its name to Paradise Inc after diversifying its operations a bit in the 90s. Paradise Inc. is the leading producer of glace (candied) fruit which is a primary ingredient of fruit cakes sold to manufacturing bakers, institutional users and supermarkets for sale during the holiday seasons of Thanksgiving and Christmas. Paradise, Inc. consists of two business segments, fruit and molded plastics. As of the most recent quarter the glace fruit segment makes up about 61% of all company sales with the plastics segment making up the remaining 39% of sales.

Candied Fruit Segment Description-Production of candied fruit, which is a basic fruitcake ingredient, is sold to manufacturing bakers, institutional users, and retailers for use in home baking. Also, based on market conditions, the processing of frozen strawberry products for sale to commercial and institutional users such as preservers, dairies drink manufacturers, etc. When PARF does sell these frozen strawberry products it is generally not a big part of its operations. **While there is no industry-wide data available, management estimates that the Company sold approximately 80% of all candied fruits and peels consumed in the U.S. during 2011.** The Company knows of two major competitors; however, it estimates that neither of these has as large a share of the market as PARF's.

Being the dominant company in your industry for years on end, owning an estimated 80% market share of the industry, and being in a niche business that makes it likely that you will not see many, if any new competitors in its market is an absolutely exceptional thing to find in any business. This combination of characteristics is something I have looked for in a company since I have started investing seriously and had not found it in any single company until now.

The demand for fruit cake materials is highly seasonal, with over 85% of sales in the glace fruits taking place in the months of September, October, and November.

In order to meet delivery requirements during this relatively short period, PARF must acquire the fruit and process it into candied fruit and peels for an estimated 10 months before this time period just to meet demand. This means that PARF has a massive build up in inventory in the quarter before the holiday months every year, and depletes its cash hoard to pay for the inventory that is needed to make sales in the last quarter of its fiscal year. These very seasonal circumstances in the fruitcake industry makes the full year results of the company, generally which come out in March of every year, the only financial report of its fiscal year that shows how truly profitable PARF has been for the preceding trailing twelve month period.

Molded Plastic Segment Description-PARF produces plastic containers for its products and other molded plastics for sale to unaffiliated customers. The molded plastics industry is very large and diverse, and PARF's management has no estimate of its total size. Many products produced by PARF are materials for its own use in the packaging of candied fruits for sale at the retail level. Outside sales represent approximately 85% of PARF's total plastics production at cost, and, in terms of the overall market, are insignificant. In the plastics molding segment of business, sales to unaffiliated customers continue to strengthen. This trend began several years ago when management shifted its focus from the sale of high volume, low profit "generics" to higher technology value added custom applications. PARF has recently started to sell packaged dried fruit as well which could become a bigger part of operations going forward.

Costs of goods sold have ranged between 71-75% of sales every year since 2003 and this year's trailing twelve month COGS is coming in at 71.98%. Despite an increase in the cost of raw materials within the fruit segment and increasing cost of resins within the Plastics segment, PARF has successfully maintained control over its production labor costs during the past year.

Management says that this can be traced directly to its previously disclosed decision and action to eliminate 15 full-time positions, reduce executive and salary wages by 15% and 10%, respectively, and rescission of a 4% merit increase awarded to hourly workers. These actions remained in place throughout 2011 and have helped reign in the cost of sales during this timeframe.

Selling, general and administrative expenses have generally taken up between 18-20% of sales over the past decade but have started to come down a bit lately from a high of 20.33% in 2002 to the trailing twelve month period being only 18.14%. This all leaves PARF's trailing twelve month operating margin at 9.86% which is much improved and is its highest operating margin in the past decade. Operating margin has actually been below 5% for most of the last decade so PARF has been able to double its operating margin in recent years. It's ROIC and ROE are a bit more volatile over the past decade but are both up over recent years and currently stand at 7.59% and 8.31% respectively over the trailing twelve month period.

My estimates of ROIC are 11.29% without goodwill and 11.09% with goodwill. One thing of note and concern is that PARF's cash conversion cycle has jumped dramatically as it stood at 160 days in its 2011 fiscal year and it now stands at 282 days in the trailing twelve month period.

This is most likely the buildup in inventory for the 2011 holiday season and may only be an aberration because of the seasonality of its business but it is something that definitely bears watching when PARF's full annual report comes out.

PARF is pretty much a family owned and operated business as out of the top five executives at the company four of them are related. The only one who seems not to be related to anyone is the CFO and treasurer Jack M. Laskowitz. Melvin S. Gordon who owns around 37% of PARF, and who is the current CEO, Chairman, and a director of the company, has been with PARF since the 1960s in various capacities. His two sons, one daughter in law, and a cousin make up the remaining five member executive team.

The group of executives has done a pretty good job over the years of managing the company and expanding its operations into the plastic industry to become more diversified which has helped the company's sales and profitability. In total insiders own right around 41% total of PARF so outside of Mr. Melvin S. Gordon the other executives own very small percentages of the company.

As with BABB in the previous chapter, PARF also has excessive executive pay in my opinion. Just the five executives in the company got paid including bonuses, in 2011 $1.551 million, or about 16% of PARF's market cap, about 6% of revenues, and about 21% of gross profit. While BABB's executive pay is worse in relation to these benchmarks, PARFs pay is still excessive in my opinion especially in relation to the company's small size of around $10 million.

Valuations

Valuations were done using PARF's 2011 10K and 2012 third quarter 10Q. All numbers are in thousands of US$, except per share information, unless otherwise noted.

Also remember that these valuations are not containing the full year's number which generally come out in March of every year, and will show a much truer picture of how the company is operating. The company's operations are extremely seasonal and in the most recent quarter PARF had to use up nearly its entire cash hoard to buy inventory. The cash should be at least partially replenished in the full year report and was standing near $7.8 million before they had to buy inventory.

Minimum Estimate of Value

EBIT Valuation

PARF has a trailing twelve month EBIT of 2,624.

5X, 8X, 11X, and 14X EBIT + cash and cash equivalents + short-term investments:

- 5X2,624=13,120/520=$25.23 per share.
- 8X2,624=20,992/520=$40.47 per share.
- 11X2,624=28,864/520=$55.51 per share.
- 14X2,624=36,736/520=$70.65 per share.

I would use the 5X EBIT estimate of intrinsic value as my minimum estimate of value for PARF.

Base Estimate of Value

Assets:	Book Value:	Reproduction Value:
Accounts Receivable	8,088	6,875
Inventories	11,664	5,832
Deferred Income Tax Asset	235	118

Prepaid Expenses & Other Current Assets	481	241
Total Current Assets	20,468	13,060
PP&E Net	4,037	2,624
Goodwill	413	0
Customer Base & Non-compete Agreement	471	236
Other Assets	233	0
Total Assets	25,622	15,920

Number of shares are 520

Reproduction Value:

- 15,920/520=$30.62 per share.

High Estimate of Value

EBIT Valuation

PARF has a trailing twelve month EBIT of 2,624.

5X, 8X, 11X, and 14X EBIT + cash and cash equivalents + short-term investments:

- 5X2,624=13,120/520=$25.23 per share.
- 8X2,624=20,992/520=$40.47 per share.
- 11X2,624=28,864/520=$55.51 per share.
- 14X2,624=36,736/520=$70.65 per share.

This time I would use the 8X EBIT value of $40.47 per share and it would be my high estimate of value for PARF.

Relative Valuations

- PARF's P/E ratio is currently 6.9 with the industry average P/E standing at 16.7. If PARF was selling at the industry average P/E it would be worth $48.40 per share.
- PARF's P/B ratio is currently 0.5 with the industry average P/B standing at 1.8. If PARF was selling at the industry average P/B it would be worth $72.00 per share.
- PARF's TEV/EBIT is currently 5.02.
- PARF's EV/EBIT is currently 4.95.

Something of major note that is not included in any of the above valuations is that:

"The Company owns its plant facilities and other properties free and clear of any mortgage obligations."

This means that PARF has some substantial hidden assets that are not fully on its books in the above valuations. I found one set of links that showed PARF's combined land, building, equipment, and properties were valued at a total of $6.6 million.

Being conservative I will use the numbers from another site which shows a more conservative set of values for the property, land, equipment, and buildings valued at an estimated $5.41 million, or $10.40 per share. This is probably a very low estimate and the combined value of the land, buildings, and equipment is most likely worth more than the $5.41 million. Discounting this amount by 40% due to where the locations are at and for the overall sake of conservatism it still brings an extra $6.24 per share to the company's valuations above.

This means the true valuations above should be: Minimum-$31.47 per share, Base-$36.86, and High-$46.71, making the company even more undervalued.

Valuation Thoughts

- By my absolute minimum estimate of value PARF is undervalued by 36%. By my base estimate of value PARF is undervalued by 46%. With my high estimate of value PARF is undervalued by 53% and is a potential double from today share price at $20 per share. Again, these valuations are not including any cash which will be at least partially replenished when the full year results come out and make PARF even more undervalued.
- PARF is undervalued by every one of my estimates of intrinsic value and relative value.
- PARF's TEV/EBIT and EV/EBIT are both under 8 which is generally the threshold I like to buy under.
- Again, all of these valuations do not contain the full year's results which are not out yet and will show a much truer picture of the company and its operations.

Customers Thoughts

PARF sells its products on its website, through Wal-Mart and Aqua Cal around the holiday seasons, smaller stores, some restaurants, and Amazon. Wal-Mart and Aqua Cal both make up a substantial portion of all sales so if either decided not to reorder it would affect the company's sales, profitability, and margins.

On Amazon like everything else that is sold on the site, customers leave reviews and generally as you can see by searching for Paradise inc, or candied fruit on Amazon, customers seem to think very highly of Paradise's products. After reading through all the reviews most people talked about the high quality of PARFs products, and how they couldn't get glace fruit in their individual local stores even sometimes around the holidays, so they had to search online for them. This could also be a potential opportunity for PARF because if there is more demand for their products that isn't being fulfilled currently, that could lead to higher sales if more people knew about them.

Some of the negative comments were about how the packaging of the product was poor and came partially crushed or even broken in some cases. In a couple of extreme cases people said that their products came with ants, bug legs, and other bug parts inside of the products.

It is hard to tell whether this is PARF's or Amazon's fault but assuming at worst that it is PARF's, this is a problem that they need to fix in the process of packaging the product and shipping it because customer reviews like this could lead to trouble in the future for the company if it were to continue to have these types of problems.

PARF has also made it to number 2 in the Top 20 Glace Fruit Websites. Only one or two of the companies on this list look to be direct competitors with PARF as most of the other companies have operations in a lot of other areas and only do a small amount of business in the glace fruit area.

Catalysts

- PARF becoming more known to people who like making fruit cakes would heighten their sales.

Pros

- PARF is the leader in its industry by far, owning an estimated 80% of all sales in the glace food market.
- PARF is in a very niche industry which should keep away competitors and its dominance intact.
- PARF is substantially undervalued by all accounts.
- PARF's management team has done a very good job running the company over the years.
- Customers generally seem to love the product.
- There could be potential for a lot more sales if more people knew about PARF's products as a lot of the customer reviews on Amazon stated that they struggled to find any glace fruit products in their local markets, sometimes even during the holiday season, and had to resort to looking online.

- PARF has nearly $500K worth of non-compete agreements signed with people to keep them from competing with PARF.
- PARF's margins are overall pretty good and I will talk about that in the conclusion article.
- PARF operates on some amount of float which I will also talk about in the finale article.
- To boost the company's margins PARF cut costs and payroll in recent years which has helped strengthen its margins.

Cons

- PARF's business is very seasonal and requires a lot of lead time so if demand drops for fruitcake during the holiday season the company's results would be highly affected.
- PARF's management and executive pay is a bit excessive in my mind.
- A few customers have had some nasty problems with PARF's products being delivered to them broken or with bug parts being in the product.
- PARF is highly dependent on Wal-Mart and Aqua Cal (Sales to these two companies make up between 20 and 25% of sales in recent years) purchasing their products for sale around the holiday season so if either one didn't reorder it would affect PARF's results.
- So far in the trailing twelve month period there has been a 120 day jump in the cash conversion cycles which is alarming. Hopefully this is just due to the lead up in having the buy inventory for

sale during the holiday season and will not be a problem after full year results come out.

Conclusion

Paradise looks like a fantastic company to own right now. It is undervalued substantially and owns a conservatively estimated $5.4 million worth of property and land that partially protects the downside of buying into PARF. It has dominated its market for years and continues to do so. Being in a very niche market and industry that it is dominating, it is unlikely that someone would come in and try to compete with them. PARF has generally good to very good margins and its operations are partially supported by float.

The continued dominance and good to very good margins lead me to believe that the company also has at least a small moat as well or at the very least by being in this extreme niche market it has helped it to gain moat like qualities due to lack of competition. I will talk about margins and float in-depth in the conclusion piece of this series. PARF's customers seem to love its products and since a lot of them complain that they cannot find glace fruit products in their local markets PARF might be able to capitalize on this with through more advertising and advertising to a wider audience that they sell their products online.

PARF does have some negatives as well with what is in my opinion excessive executive pay, heavy reliance on two customers, some previous problems with its packaging, and it's very seasonal market but up to this point PARF looks like a very exceptional company to invest in as the positives far outweigh the negatives in my opinion.

Next up is the conclusion to the previous two chapters and the analysis explanation where I will explain my thought process and how it was decided which one was a better company to own at the time. There will also be a bit of an update about BABB's recent decision to keep outside investors from making positive changes at it.

Chapter 14: BABB Vs PARF Conclusion, March 2013. Margin Comparison, Earnings Yield, Making Tough Decisions, Cash Conversion Cycle, and Protection of Downside.

"Successful investors tend to be unemotional, allowing the greed and fear of others to play into their hands. By having confidence in their own analysis and judgment, they respond to market forces not with blind emotion but with calculated reason. Successful investors, for example, demonstrate caution in frothy markets and steadfast conviction in panicky ones. Indeed, the very way an investor views the market and it's price fluctuations is a key factor in his or her ultimate investment success or failure." Seth Klarman

Margin Comparison

	BABB Margins	PARF Margins
Gross Margin TTM	96.2	28
Gross Margin 5 Year Average	88.64	26.32
Gross Margin 10 Year Average	79.25	26.37
Op Margin TTM	17.9	9.9
Op Margin 5 Year Average	-0.76	5.9
Op Margin 10 Year Average	6.75	4.24

ROE TTM		15.51%	8.31
ROE 5 Year Average		-2.80%	5.064
ROIC TTM		14.51%	7.59
ROIC 5 Year Average		-17.20%	9.278
My ROIC TTM With Goodwill Using Total Obligations		24.39%	11.09%
My ROIC TTM Without Goodwill Using Total Obligations		88.11%	11.29%
Earnings Yield EBIT/TEV		14.15%	19.91%

FCF/Sales TTM	15.02	-5.55
FCF/Sales 5 Year Average	13.296	3.116
FCF/Sales 10 Year Average	15.658	2.828
P/B Current	1.47	0.55
Insider Ownership Current	N/A	N/A
My EV/EBIT Current	6.58	4.95
My TEV/EBIT Current	7.07	5.02
Working Capital TTM	1 mil	15.62 mil
Working Capital 5 Yr	1 mil	12.2 mil

Avg				
Book Value Per Share Current			0.43	39.72
Book Value Per Share 5 Yr Avg			0.498	36.254
Total Executive Compensation as a % of Sales			26.17%	6.00%
Total Executive Compensation as a % of Gross Margin			26.17%	21.00%
Total Executive Compensation as a % of Market Cap			15.91%	16.00%
Total Executive Compensation as a % of Total Enterprise			19.65%	11.47%

Value		
Debt Comparisons:		
Total Debt as a % of Balance Sheet TTM	3.05%	10.12%
Total Debt as a % of Balance Sheet 5 year Average	4.88%	2.64%
Current Assets to Current Liabilities	2.17	4.25
Total Debt to Equity	4.84%	12.56%
Total Debt to Total Assets	3.74%	11.70%

Total Obligations and Debt/EBIT	30.36%	98.78%
Costs Of Goods Sold As A % Of Balance Sheet TTM	0	71.98%
Costs Of Goods Sold As A % Of Balance Sheet 5 Year Avg	10.60%	73.54%

Keep in mind while looking at these margins that PARF is an extremely seasonal business so its margins will probably look different in a month when the company reports its full year results, and probably for the better, at least marginally.

Margin Thoughts

- BABB's gross margins are phenomenal which should be expected from a company whose only business right now is to sit and collect royalty and franchise fees.
- BABB has superior operating margins, ROE, and ROIC in comparison to PARF. Again, this should be expected with its business model in comparison to PARFs.
- PARFs earnings yield, in this case EBIT/TEV, is superior to BABBs by about 25%.

- Since this is a new metric I am using I went back and calculated this for the two most recent companies I have bought stock in, STRT and BOBS, and here is how the earnings yields compare: 1) STRT-20.79% 2) PARF-19.91% 3) BOBS-14.80%, 4) BABB-14.15%.
- Earnings yield is a rough estimate of the kind of return you may be able to expect in the future by buying the company at its current price and is compared to the current 10 year treasury yield. I have seen prominent value investors say they like to buy companies with earnings yields at least 3X to 4X higher than the 10 year yield. Current 10 year treasury yield is 2% currently so all of these companies surpass the 3X to 4X benchmark with Strattec leading the way.
- As I talked about in both of the previous articles both companies ROIC could be higher if executive pay and overall payroll were not at the excessive levels that they are at currently.
- BABB's FCF/Sales is exceptional and PARF's is currently negative but that should change once the full year results are announced.
- PARF's P/B ratio is incredibly low as the company is selling for only half of its current book value and this value is likely a bit undervalued which would mean PARF is currently selling at even a lower true P/B.
- PARF's current estimated book value per share is around $40 per share and the company is selling at $22 a share currently.

- Both companies are selling for EV/EBIT and TEV/EBIT ratios fewer than 8 which are again what I want them to be under.
- Both companies executive pay is excessive in my eyes especially BABBs. Remember also about BABB is that its entire payroll structure is inflated and the above calculations are not including overall payroll. Including overall payroll for BABB and its payroll and executive pay take up more than 50% of the company's gross margin; absolutely insane in my opinion.
- Both companies have minimal debt and have stellar balance sheets.
- PARF's total obligations and debt/EBIT is too high in my opinion but again this should be at least somewhat corrected when the full year numbers are released.
- COGS for BABB are completely irrelevant now that they do not directly operate any of its restaurants.
- PARFs COGS has come down over recent years which have been why margins have risen in recent years.

Float Analysis Comparison

BABB Analysis

Financial assets: Cash and cash equivalents=1,256+prepaid expenses of 66+ deferred income taxes 248=1,570.

Operating assets: Accounts receivable of 86+inventories of 27+other current assets of 393+net property, plant, and equipment of 11+ goodwill of 1,494 + intangible assets of 505 + other long term assets of 4=2,520.

- Total assets=4,090

Liabilities:

- Equity=3,158
- Debt=125
- Float=accounts payable of 14+deferred revenues of 71+other current liabilities of 722=807

Total liabilities=923

Float/operating assets=807/2,520=32.02%. Float is supporting 32.02% of operating assets.

Pretax profits/total assets=ROA

- 434.15/4,090=10.62%

Pretax profits/ (total assets-float) = Levered ROA

- 434.15/3,283=13.22%

PARF Analysis

For this analysis I used PARFs 2011 full year numbers because of the extreme seasonality of its business and to get an idea of what the company may look like when its 2012 full year numbers come out in March.

Financial assets: Cash and cash equivalents=7,469+deferred income taxes of 235+ prepaid expenses of 295=7,999.

Operating assets: Accounts receivable of 2,579+inventories of 6,197+net property, plant, and equipment of 4,184 + goodwill of 413 + intangible assets of 566 + other long-term assets of 223=14,162.

- Total assets=22,161

Liabilities:

- Equity=19,734
- Debt=313
- Float=accounts payable of 359+taxes payable of 371+accrued liabilities of 1,218+deferred tax liabilities of 166=2,114

Total liabilities=2,427

Float/operating assets=2,114/14,162=14.93%. Float is supporting 14.93% of operating assets.

Pretax profits/total assets=ROA

- 1,929.29/22,161=8.71%

Pretax profits/ (total assets-float) = Levered ROA

- 1,929.29/20,047=9.62%

Float Thoughts

- BABBs float is supporting more of the company's operations than PARFs is.
- Other than the directly above, the companies have pretty similar ROAs and amount of float and neither one has a distinct advantage in this area.

Conclusion

Combining the above with the information in the previous two chapters I have come to some conclusions about the two companies. BABB has the better business model that leads to generally higher margins and minimal work for the company. PARF has dominated its market for years, it still does, and it has found a small niche that has led to great profitability over the years. Both companies have excessive executive pay in my opinion that if lowered could help each company's operations become more profitable. Both companies look like potentially good investment candidates right now so how have I decided which is the better one to buy into at the current time with the companies being very even overall?

1. BABB has a lot of competition in its industry, has had to close restaurants, and has lost its miniscule market share to other companies. Meanwhile PARF has only a few minor competitors and dominates its industry with an estimated 80% share of its market. Another major positive is that it dominates a very niche industry which should keep competition out of its market, further cementing its hold on market share.
2. PARF owns land, building, and property that are conservatively estimated to be worth about $10.40 per share and partially protects the company's downside. BABB has no such downside protection and if it continues to lose franchisees, shareholders are completely out of luck and could stand to lose all of their investment in the company.

Having stated the above I have bought into PARF for the portfolios that I manage.

Update About BABB:

The two companies were generally very close but as you know by now I am a very conservative investor who likes the downside protected as much as possible when buying into a company and PARF having hard saleable assets was the main thing that pushed me to buy them instead of BABB and boy am I glad that decision was made.

After I posted the original article about BABB I continued to follow the company closely because I still thought it was a potentially good investment.

I started to become even more frustrated with its management as time went on and posted on my blog that I was trying to get a group of value investors together that could become activist within the company to make changes for the betterment of all shareholders, mainly pertaining to lowering the overall payroll of the company.

A couple of months after that was posted about on my blog, BABB's management enacted what have been termed poison pill provisions in its bylaws to keep outside investors from acquiring a big enough chunk of the company to make any changes. These so-called poison pill provisions are outlined on my blog where I link to the page that was talking about these new bylaws and you can find them by searching BABB.

The cliffs notes version is that a couple of months after the original article, and subsequent posts about potentially becoming an activist investor within the company, its management enacted what they deem a "Stockholder's Rights Plan." This so-called Stockholder's Rights Plan allows the company to issue rights to current shareholders if someone buys 15% of its shares (20% in the case of an institution) to "Protect Shareholders best interests" from outside investors. These rights would be issued to shareholders as of May 13th, 2013 if someone were to purchase 15 or 20% of BABB and looks to essentially be a way to keep outsiders from attempting to make any changes within the company.

There is also this amazing line from the announcement:

"BAB's Board of Directors may redeem the Rights for $0.001 per Right at any time before an event that causes the Rights to become exercisable. The Rights will expire on the third anniversary date of the Agreement, unless the Rights have previously been redeemed by the Board of Directors."

This gives a further advantage to insiders over regular shareholders because the board of directors can start accumulating more shares with these stock rights before anyone even attempts to buy a big chunk of BABB. Obviously the above was shocking to me.

It looks that current BABB management likes the status quo of taking giant payrolls, losing market share, and losing restaurant count and does not want to have things shaken up by outside investors who may want to lower overall pay, help the company become more profitable, and help the company grow again.

This is my first experience with a company doing something like this but knew it would eventually happen because a lot of nano caps are managed by a very small number of insiders who effectively control the company. It is still surprising and disappointing that they would do something like this, but apparently they would rather just keep milking the company instead of putting some of that excessive pay towards growing the company or growing earnings and cash flow. Suffice it to say that I am glad I did not buy into BABB as this shows that its management does not care about the best interests of shareholders.

Another thing that was shocking to me was that while BABB's restaurant count dropped by 20% since 2007, its management has increased its pay and the overall company payroll. Also in this time frame insiders have sold about 10% of the company's stock that they once owned. This means that the company was taking more money to give to themselves while the pool of profits was continually being lowered. This was another major reason why I chose PARF over BABB because when PARF was having problems several years ago its management cut costs and payroll for everyone, including management, to help regain profitability which made the company much healthier overall. Since BABB has no downside protection from saleable assets like PARF does this means that BABB shareholders could potentially lose everything if it continues on the same route that it is currently taking.

Above is why a lot of even veteran investors do not like investing in these very small companies that are controlled by only a few insiders as they can pretty much do as they please if they control enough of the company. You have to make sure that you trust management enough to buy into these kinds of companies and sometimes hope for the best and hope that they do not do something like BABB's management did. As have stated before; it doesn't matter how undervalued a company is or how amazing its balance sheet is if you are not able to trust that management has shareholders best interests at heart.

Analysis Explanation:

Customer reviews are something that I have added recently because it makes a lot of sense to at least get an idea of what a company's customers think of it and how that can affect a company. You can find reviews for pretty much anything online now and if you decide to read them it could lead you to answer some questions about the companies you are researching like it did with my question about why BABB's restaurant count has continued to drop over the years.

By searching customer reviews online I found it was possibly due to its perceived lack of customer friendliness and perceived overpriced products which could have led to customers not going to those restaurants any more. It may also lead you to a potential opportunity for growth at a company like when researching PARF and found out that people couldn't find glace fruit products in a lot of their local groceries. This is a very valuable tool and I now always look at customer reviews for every company I do full research on now.

Cash Conversion Cycle or CCC is a metric that expresses the length of time, in days, that it takes for a company to convert resources into cash flow. This metric looks at the amount of time needed to sell inventory, the amount of time needed to collect receivables, and the length of time the company is afforded to pay its bills without incurring penalties. This is calculated as follows: CCC=DIO+DSO-DPO.

- DIO represents days inventory outstanding.
- DSO represents days sales outstanding.
- DPO represents days payable outstanding.

Generally the lower this number the better because the lower this number is the faster a company can convert its inventory into sales and the faster sales convert into cash which then starts the cycle over again. This number can also be negative which means that the company completes this cycle faster than they have to buy inventory.

This is a very good thing as it essentially means that a company's customers are buying and paying for products before the company has to pay for them. This metric is most useful when evaluating retail or retail like companies. The cash conversion cycle should be compared to previous years and you should look at the CCC over a 5-10 year period. Generally you would like to see this number decrease over time. If it increases steadily over time or jumps drastically all the sudden the company could be having some problems selling its products or it may mean that the company is doing something untoward.

I would highly recommend reading Financial Shenanigans: How To Detect Accounting Gimmicks and Fraud in Financial Reports to understand the CCC better and how this and other metrics can be manipulated by management to hide problems within a company's financial reports. With a very seasonal business like PARF this number can also jump dramatically in a short amount of time due to the buildup of product over many months without making sales and should not cause major concern unless the number stays inflated after the seasonal sales period.

PARF is in the declining fruit cake industry and everyone I know either hates fruit cake or has never tried it so why would anyone want to own a company who operates in a declining industry and makes the glace fruit that goes into fruit cakes? There are several reasons why I bought into PARF and feel that it is a good investment: The company is extremely undervalued, it has hard saleable assets if it gets into any trouble, it operates in a very niche industry where it has remained profitable for years, and it dominates its very niche industry with an estimated 80% share of the market.

Frankly I do not care if a company is in a declining market if it has these characteristics because my downside is protected if the industry declines further, and PARF will be hurt the least, last the longest, and make the most profit if the fruit cake industry continues to decline as the smaller competitors would be the first to either leave the market, go bankrupt, or be bought out. This means that PARF could stay profitable for years if that did happen and possibly expand its dominance in its industry. To me this makes sense, to other investors I have talked with whom I respect it does not.

This is again why you must do your own research and come to your own conclusions. Even among nano cap value investors (A very small group of people by the way) there is great disagreement about what is a good investment and what is not and only you can decide if a company is a good investment for you at that particular time or not.

The valuing of PARF's assets that have been fully depreciated is pretty much like valuing something like DOLE's assets that are still on its books. You do research and try to find the best estimate of value that you can and possibly discount that amount if you think that needs to happen for the sake of conservatism.

The main difference between assets that are still on a balance sheet as is the case with DOLE, and a company's assets like PARF's who have been almost fully depreciated is that if a company's assets have been fully depreciated they are not on the company's books and will probably not be talked about in great detail in a company's filings. It required quite a bit of digging to find estimates of value for PARF's properties.

When you find a reasonable estimate of value for the kind of land assets and property that PARF has can be very lucrative as most investors will not take the time to look for the value of these things because it can take many hours of work. This can pay off big time though if you choose to look for the value of these assets as they can sometimes be worth a lot of money.

As you saw in the chapter on PARF it was selling for about $22 a share at the time of the original article and I found a very conservatively valued $10+ per share worth of land, equipment, buildings, etc, that were only mentioned in a couple of lines in its annual report because they had been almost completely depreciated. Another line of great importance here was that PARF stated they held several properties that were paid off and completely free of any mortgage or rent. So not only are these hidden properties worth a conservative $10+ per share, but they do not have to pay any mortgage or rent on them leading to further cost savings.

Again this kind of research into a company's hidden assets can be very lucrative for the person who is willing to look for them and can lead you to finding substantial value within a company. Most other people including professional investors will not look for the value of these kinds of assets because they don't want to take the time to look for it. The goal here is to have any kind of legal informational advantage you can over other investors. You can achieve that in situations like this just by doing a little more work than most other people are willing to do and you can potentially be paid handsomely for it.

Chapter 15: Conclusion: Challenge To You, How I Do Research, Mindset, Patience, When To Sell A Company.

"Nobody ever takes note of [my advice], because it's not the answer they wanted to hear. What they want to hear is 'Here's how you get an agent, here's how you write a script,' . . . but I always say, **'Be so good they can't ignore you.'** " Steve Martin

"Unless you can watch your stock holdings decline by 50% without becoming panic-stricken, you should not be in the stock market." Warren Buffett

I originally started my value investing blog, Value Investing Journey, and now this book, because of frustrations when I could not find any other single site, group of sites, or books that talked about the things that have been talked about in this book. Most value investing blogs will talk about the companies they think are good investments, show some basic valuations, talk about why they think the particular company is a good investment, and go into a little detail about the company's operations.

This approach is fine if you already know how to value and evaluate companies but if you do not you are in for a very long, often times frustrating journey, through the infinite internet until you finally piece enough disparate information together to start the process of learning and implementing valuation techniques, thought processes, and how to properly gauge whether a company is a potentially good investment into your own repertoire.

The Value Investing Journey blog was originally started to keep a journal of my thoughts and valuation and analysis articles so that I could see what I was learning, how fast I was learning, and come back to that later to see how far I had come in the time since I started the blog.

There was one other major reason it was started, and why I eventually decided to write this book as well. I wanted to help newer to intermediate level investors who like me could not, or did not, want to go to a big time university to learn the techniques that have been shown and have talked about in this book so that you could jump-start your own investing journey a lot faster than the nearly 5 years it has taken me to gain the knowledge that I have.

Throughout this book and on the accompanying blog, I have shown and given you access to all the best information I have learned from that took thousands of hours and nearly five years to put together. I have shown you how to do the valuation techniques for yourself, talked about my investment thought processes, why I did what I did, and have given you all the tools and necessary information so that you can become a truly excellent value investor without going to college and without having to spend potentially tens or hundreds of thousands of dollars. While the potential money savings are great I also think that by following this book and the accompanying blog that you can save potentially thousands of hours of your precious time as well.

Now that we are coming to the end of this book the first thing I want to do is to tell you that if you have followed this book closely; have practiced the techniques, learned the terms, and have started learning from the some of the outside resources listed throughout this book and on the accompanying blog, that I guarantee you will now know more about how to value and evaluate whether a company is a good or bad investment better than most MBA's and professional equity analysts while also saving hundreds of hours of time and tens of thousands of dollars. It does not matter how much knowledge you have gained though because if you do not apply the knowledge through practice you will not retain any of this information and you will not grow and get better as an investor.

When originally getting serious about investing I used to just read books and websites constantly while never taking any time to practice the techniques that I was learning. I never took the time to practice the techniques I was learning because I thought that I still didn't know enough to start evaluating a company properly. Finally I realized that the reason I wasn't improving at all was because I was not practicing valuing companies and was not retaining any of the information that I was learning from because of not practicing. Once again; if you do not practice what you are learning you will not retain the information, you will waste a lot of time having to relearn things, and you will not improve as an investor. Be confident in your abilities and go out there and keep practicing and getting better. If you are serious about becoming a much better investor faster, valuing and analyzing companies is not a once every month or so exercise. You need to practice constantly to keep getting better and to develop your own thought processes about what you think makes a company an excellent investment. No one else can answer that all important question for you, but you.

I highly recommend starting a value investing blog where you talk about your ideas and post your analysis for everyone to see. Starting my blog was the number one factor in me getting better as an investor. Starting a blog is a great way to keep track of your progress to see how much better you have gotten over time.

It is also a very valuable way to keep track of what has and has not worked in your analysis and thought processes because you can always go back to see what you need to improve on and where your thought process and analysis may have been flawed so that you can go back and fix those problems. It is also a very good way to keep track of things you have done right so that you can keep improving on those thought processes and analysis and keep integrating more of those positive results into your evaluations.

You may have noticed that I have never once in this book said that I will guarantee that you will make a lot of money from the knowledge in this book once you learn the techniques and valuations. In my opinion people who guarantee those kinds of things are selling you snake oil, should be viewed with skepticism, and should be ignored. You can put together a great valuation and analysis article and the company's stock may end up going south fast and you could end up losing a lot of money even if you have a bulletproof analysis put together. You may also not put very much work into valuing and analyzing a company but end up getting lucky by the company that you just bought into getting bought out for a quick double or triple. Investing is a lot like poker where over the long-term luck does not play a very big role and generally the better players end up at the final tables a lot more often. But like in poker as in investing luck plays a pretty big role in the short-term.

For example you could find an exceptional company that is undervalued and you see it as a potential double or triple once its full value is realized. You could put a ton of work into the analysis, write-up a great analysis article, buy into the company and then boom the next day the stock market crashes and you are automatically down 50% the day after you bought into this company. This is why you must do proper research into an investment decision and put a lot of work into analyzing companies because if you did your proper due diligence and you still feel that the company is an exceptional investment this would be a perfect time to buy more of that particular company and now you would think that instead of a potential double or triple the company could turn into a four bagger plus.

The goal of this book is to get you to be a better investor for the long-term so that over time luck will even out and your skill will show. I have seen very prominent investors say that you should be happy if 4-6 out of 10 of your investments turn out well. The goal of this book is to give you the basis to become a .400 to .600 hitter when finding investments.

This book is about teaching you the techniques, valuations, and basic framework of how to become an excellent investor. These unfortunately are not the most important factors that will decide if you are to become an excellent value investor however.

Thought process, temperament, patience, having confidence in what you are doing, and willingness and dedication to continue to learn and get better are what is going to determine if you become a fantastic investor. It does not matter how much technique and knowledge of how to value and evaluate companies you have, although this will help greatly, if you are impatient, do not work to develop the proper thought processes for yourself, do not work to continually get better, and do not have the proper temperament you will most likely end up being a very bad investor and losing money. The following traits are of utmost importance if you want to become an excellent value investor.

Thought/Decision Making Process: Value investing is generally a very solitary endeavor where you put in a lot of hours of work by yourself to find one company out of hundreds that you think is going to be a good investment. During those probably dozens or hundreds of hours of research into one company you will have to determine a plethora of things on your own: If you think the company has a moat, if the company has a moat is it a big one and is it sustainable over the long-term, is it in a dying industry, is it a growing industry, are the companies margins and sales growing or declining, will the company be around in five years, can you trust management, is the company dominant or going to be dominant in its industry, and on and on.

The above examples are only a few of the many things you need to think about and to ask and determine for yourself before investing in a company. Even if you do have a mentor that you can bounce ideas and thoughts off of and ask questions of (I would highly recommend finding someone you can bounce ideas off of because it will help you become a much better investor faster) still only you can answer investment specific questions for yourself and how these things integrate into your own personal idea of what makes a potentially great investment. Outside of learning the terms, techniques, valuations, and how to evaluate a company, developing a proper thought and investment process for yourself is going to be the greatest investment you will make that will pay dividends far into the future. The faster you determine the best thought processes for yourself and how to incorporate those into an excellent investment analysis, the faster you will become a much better investor.

Patience, Temperament, and Confidence:
I combined these three together because they are all needed in concert to become an excellent investor. Having patience in most things outside of investing is not the same thing as having patience when you buy into a company and its stock goes down 50% shortly after you bought into it. This is why you need patience, the proper temperament, and confidence all together.

I will go back to the example I used earlier to hit this point home. Let's say that after reading this book and evaluating a few companies you find a company that is undervalued, has a stable balance sheet, quite a bit of cash on hand, not a lot of debt, is growing efficiently, has fantastic margins, and has at least a small moat. You think the company looks like a potential double or triple from today's prices and its downside is protected at least partially by some land that it owns. All things look good in your eyes and you can't believe that the company is so undervalued so you decide to buy into it and put 20% of your portfolio into buying stock in the company. A few days after you buy into the company the stock market crashes and the stock loses 50% of its value, what do you do? Panic and sell the company because you are afraid you are going to lose more money, wait and do nothing, remain calm and buy more?

If you did your proper due diligence this is when it pays to have written your ideas so you can go back and look at the reasons you bought in the first place. Again, I highly recommend starting an investment journal or blog because it is a very easy way to keep track of your ideas. If the company is still in sound shape financially and all that is different is that the company's stock has dropped by 50% what would you do?

Until you can answer this question truthfully to yourself you should not be investing any real money. If you still have confidence in your article/report you wrote and you still think the company is financially sound and will survive the market crash you would either want to do nothing or buy more shares. Patience, proper temperament to remain calm when things are going crazy, remaining unemotional and analytical, and having confidence are especially important when something like this happens and if you do not have enough of these traits you need to work on improving them if you want to become an excellent value investor.

Willingness and Dedication to Continue to Learn and Willpower: I have always loved learning about everything, have constantly sought out knowledge on my own, and have always pushed to constantly improve at every aspect of my life. This is one of the reasons I find investing so intellectually stimulating is because there is always something new to learn, something else to get better at, and always another company or situation to research. If you do not have the willingness and dedication to always learn, get better, and evolve your thought processes you will not grow as an investor. Because value investing is a very solitary activity you will have to push and dedicate yourself to constantly getting better on your own. This can kind of be like working out in some ways because if you truly want to improve yourself you will need to get up and do the work even on days you do not want to.

When To Sell A Company's Stock

Even though I talked about this a little bit earlier in the book I wanted to expound on my decision-making thought process when selling a company. Thank you to those readers who asked that I write about this because this is something I struggled with mightily when starting investing.

I have read many times that you should not only come up with a sound buying process but also a sound selling process as well. For the first several years of my value investing journey I completely ignored this advice when it came to selling and took each sell decision on a case by case basis with no actual decision-making processes intact other than what I thought about the company on that particular day. This worked for a while but caused some major short-term problems for me once fully invested in my personal portfolio.

Before talking about that situation we need to go back to see why I was fully invested at the time though. Once I started getting serious about becoming a much better value investor and refining my processes and techniques I started to find more and more companies that were undervalued that I wanted to buy.

However, I still owned some companies from before doing any real research, most of which I was in the red on, and didn't want to sell them before I made my money back. As you can imagine, that worked out horribly as you will see below.

Do not buy companies without doing research and do not hold on to bad investments just because you want to make your money back, it will end up costing you even more money in the long run like it did for me. Do not be stubborn like I was.

Soon after I got serious about digging into companies I found Dole which was talked about in chapter 8. That chapter was based on my second article about Dole but I actually wrote my first article about them in late May and early June of 2012 describing why I thought they were massively undervalued and how they could sell or spin-off some of their assets to get rid of their massive debt load which would help unlock that undervaluation. I bought the company in that time frame for the portfolios that I manage but not in my personal portfolio because I was fully invested and in my stubbornness did not want to sell companies that I was losing money on as I described above.

Luckily for the portfolios I manage within 100 days of buying into them, Dole announced that it was going to sell its worldwide operations to Itochu which would enable them to pay off all of their debt if they chose to do so. The cost basis of the shares I owned of Dole in those portfolios was $8.50 a share. Dole's shares had been slowly rising over time but after this announcement came out it sent the share price over $15 at one point and I ended up selling the shares in the portfolios that I manage around $14.50 per share for a gain of 66% in 104 days.

This still hurts a lot more than any actual losses I have had because I put together a good analysis, did the proper due diligence, the investment thesis came together like I thought it would, but I was too stubborn and emotional to sell those other companies so that the situation could be taken advantage of in my portfolio. What would you hate more, losing a little bit of money on a bad company that you do not want to own, or losing out on a nearly 70% gain in around a 100 days like I did? Unfortunately I know which hurts more. Do not let your emotions take control of your investment decisions.

After this I decided that I needed to have solid sell decision processes in place so that I would no longer agonize over my sell decisions, help take emotion out of the equation, and alleviate my inherent stubbornness.

Instead of doing things on a case by case basis which would let emotions make the decisions for me, I now have a very regimented sell decision-making process and will sell in the following cases <u>no matter what</u>:

1. If I find another company that is a better company to own; more undervalued, bigger margin of safety, better profitability, etc than the company I'm thinking about selling.
2. If my original investment thesis turns out to be wrong.
3. If the company's management starts doing things that I do not like.
4. If I buy into a company and it reaches the higher end of my valuation range quickly.
5. If a company I own reaches the higher end of my valuation range and the market as a whole is overvalued.

If a company doesn't meet any of those criteria I generally plan to hold onto the company for years if my original investment thesis continues to play out. I also recommend revaluing each company you own at least twice annually as well because its valuation will change when its new quarterly and annual reports come out.

You need to factor the new numbers into your valuations to get a new valuation range when its operations and profitability change over time. For example if a company continues to improve its operations and profitability over time, the company could remain perennially undervalued and become further undervalued over time. Search Brazil Fast Food on my blog for an updated valuation of that company for a great example of the previous. Obviously the reverse will be true also.

Biggest lessons from this section: Do not be like how I was as an early "investor", do not let emotions and stubbornness rule your decisions, and come up with your own very sound, regimented buy AND sell decision-making processes, the earlier the better.

Challenge To You and How I Do Research

The first thing I recommend after reading this book is to find a company you find interesting for some reason, read its annual, quarterly, and proxy reports, and value and evaluate the company. THE ONLY WAY you are going to improve as a value investor is if you constantly practice techniques and valuations, work on your thought and investment process, and work on your patience, temperament, and confidence as you get better.

When I say constantly practice I do not mean just doing the same thing over and over like most people do, is very easy, and is sometimes even fun. When I say practice I mean deliberate practice where you constantly push yourself to learn new things and constantly look for ways to improve by going back over your previous articles and reports to see where you may have made some errors. This kind of practice is not easy, generally isn't fun, and takes a lot more time. If you truly want to become an excellent value investor though you must practice deliberately and not just keep doing the same things over and over. For some examples of deliberate practice search my blog or Google with the words Deliberate Practice.

The way I do research has probably been the area that has changed and evolved the most since starting to invest. I used to put together very detailed stock screeners on places like finviz.com looking for companies that had good-looking ratios and that was about it. I looked for things like a high current ratio, high margins, growing revenues, high insider ownership, etc and ended up wasting a lot of time sifting through poor companies because I didn't have a defined and repeatable way of searching for companies.

Now I follow a very regimented research strategy that has paid off by saving me a lot of time and has helped me find better companies faster. Instead of doing my full research on a company that had good-looking ratios, I now follow a three-step process that discards a lot of companies off the bat and saves a lot of time. Before we get into the details of what I do, I want to tell you that this is just what works for me and it may not work for you. You need to find whatever works best for you but I wanted to share how I do research because I get the question relatively often.

The first thing I do now is put together a very basic stock screen with only a few criteria instead of the 10+ individual criteria I used to use each time. All of this is based on finviz.com. I use very basic search criteria in the screens now like recent positive insider buys, if it has a P/B below 2, and it has a market cap below $300 million. Sometimes using more sometimes less, but generally this is the criteria I now use to start with.

I also consider the amount of shares that insiders own, if any analysts are covering the company, if a company has had recent bad or good news, if the company is under strategic review, and a lot of other criteria as well but those are a lot more subjective to my preferences than anything. Recent insider buys are always something I like to see because insiders know more about the company than anyone and if they are buying it usually means they expect the company to do well over time or they think the company is undervalued. Make sure that the insider buys are actually buys in the open market and not just the awarding of options or shares by the company. You can do this by looking at the company's form 4 releases which can usually be found on the company's site or on Morningstar.com. In all honesty I would love to see a company that has P/B below 1 but I use 2 as my cut off. I used to use a P/B of 1 and below as the cut off but that left very few companies to look through. Now that I am more confident I concentrate almost exclusively on small and nano cap companies because a lot of investors and analysts do not look at these smaller companies. This is different from large caps where sometimes dozens or hundreds of entities are following a company. If you are interested in special situations you can use sites like stockspinoffs.com as well. I also find investment ideas from other value investing blogs, insidermonkey.com, Seeking Alpha, GuruFocus, etc.

With the above criteria from the stock screen I usually end up with a list of between 50-350 companies to look into. After that I discard Chinese companies because of my previous horrible experience with Chinese small caps. I also discard financials except insurance companies, pharmaceuticals, and mining/natural resource companies because I do not understand how to value or analyze those companies. After discarding those companies I end up with a list of between 30-150 companies usually.

When I get to this point I go one by one using Morningstar.com or yahoo finance to look at things like insider ownership, what the company does for business, how healthy the company's balance sheet is, its profitability, any positive or negative news, or if I find a company to be interesting for some reason, to determine which companies I am going to do further research on. Using my personal criteria for what I look for in an investment (Again, this is something you will have to figure out for yourself) I narrow that list of usually as many as 150 companies down to fewer than 5 that I start minimal research on.

For each of the as many as 5 companies remaining I download each company's most recent annual, quarterly, and proxy report, read through those reports and take notes on them.

At this point I will discard more companies, sometimes all of them if I find enough things about the companies that bother me. Things like related party transactions, decreasing profitability, excessive management pay, expensive law suits, expiring patents, debt filled balance sheets, etc. If I discard all the companies at this point I then adjust the stock screener and start the research all the way over from the beginning going through several hundred companies again. I also may look for things like spin offs, companies that are experiencing good or bad news, or a company that I find interesting for some reason.

If I find a company or companies that I still like after reading the most recent financial reports of a company I then value the company or companies and analyze its float to see if they are undervalued and if they could potentially have a moat. At this point I usually end up discarding all the companies because they are not undervalued enough or their margins are not good enough for me to invest in. I will then adjust my search criteria again and start looking through potentially hundreds of companies to find more to research.

If I do find a company that is undervalued or supremely interesting still, this is where I end up doing my full amount of research and analysis and generally end up writing an article.

At this point I download an annual report for at least each of the past five years (10+ years if they go back that far) and read every one of those annual reports and take a lot of notes to see if a company has had problems in the past, how they went through the previous recession to get an idea of how they may react in another worst case scenario, how they came out of those problems and got better, and how the company's operations have evolved over time. I take notes about margins, debt, cash levels, profitability, revenue, float, total obligations and commitments, how a company's operations have changed over time, and how these things have changed over the years. I also research the company's competitors, usually reading at least a few of their annual reports, taking notes on their margins, debt, cash levels, profitability, revenue, float, etc to compare the companies together over a long time period to see how they stack up against each other and to see who is at least on a relative basis the most undervalued. While doing research on competitors keep in mind that these can also turn into potential investments if they end up having better margins, better profitability, and are more undervalued than the company you are analyzing as well. I read proxy reports to see what executive and management pay is, if there are any red flags, who owns 5%+ of the company, and to find out if management is exceptional. I also search Google to see if there have been any new developments within the company since their last annual or quarterly report came out to see if there are any new things that need to be factored into the analysis. Those are the main things I look for but I also look at some other things I consider to be more minor but can potentially have major relevance as well like industry trends, if the overall market is over or undervalued, how the company may do over the long-term, etc. At this point I usually end up writing an article because by this point I have put in well over 100 hours discarding companies, researching, valuing, and analyzing the company that I did find that was interesting or undervalued and its competitors.

Even after all of this work I still may not end up buying into a company. You need to keep an open mind and let the numbers and your analysis take you where they may and not be boxed into wanting to buy into a company just because you put a lot of hours into researching said company. When I get to this point I still end up buying into just over half of the companies I do full research on because they ended up not being as good of an investment as I thought they would be.

If you think value investing is easy and not time-consuming you are very wrong. By the time I write an article about a company, I have discarded a few hundred companies, and spent a hundred hours plus discarding companies, researching, analyzing, valuing, and comparing a company or companies to their competitors, still to only have a little better than a 50% chance of buying into a company.

This seems insane, and it probably is to some degree, but if you want to truly be an excellent value investor you need to research as many companies as possible. Around the world there are tens of thousands of companies that you can research and you can only find investments that fit your particular criteria if you put in the work to find them. This obviously takes a lot of personal drive, will, and passion. Value investing is probably something you cannot get excellent at if you do not have passion for it and actually like digging into companies.   Reading companies annual reports fascinates and relaxes me and is treated like a kind of treasure hunt. Most people, including most professional investors, find it boring and just are investing because it is good way to make money. If you do not have the drive, will, and passion to do hundreds of hours of work, while still only having a little better than a 50% chance of finding a company to buy into, this is probably not a very good way to spend your time and you should probably let someone like me who loves doing this manage your investments so that you can free up your time to do things you like and want to do.

Websites, Books, Articles, etc Information to Learn From.

Because it would take up to much space here I have listed the most important books and sites on the Recommended Reading page on my blog, valueinvestingjourney.com. If you see anything else you want to know you can use the keyword search bar on the front page of the blog to enter a search for information there.

For example if you want to learn more about moats and float then you would enter either moat or float into the search bar and that will take you to a list of posts where I have talked about those subjects. If you can't find something that you want to on my blog you should use Google. If it is an investing related term you need help understanding I cannot recommend investopedia.com enough.

Something that I have not mentioned on my blog yet or in this book is another way to get free/cheap books and information. This book and the knowledge I have gained have exclusively been from books, sites, articles, etc that I have either found online or that I have seen recommended. Books can be very expensive but a lot of them can be found free online and I have links to some free book on the site.

To find those posts search free books or books in the search bar. If you cannot find a particular book that you want to learn from free you should of course pay for it to support authors like me or you can use a site like paperbackswap.com. I have used the site for years and have acquired a lot of my books from there. There is no charge to join and no charge to get books from others on the site. The way to receive books is that you have to send out books to people who are requesting those books. The only cost to you to receive books is shipping and handling of the books you send out. When those people receive the book you sent them you will receive a credit that you can then use to request books of your own. They also have a market place where you can buy books at a discount as well. Another way to find free/cheap books is from Kindle daily deals. This is something you will probably want to be alerted about from Amazon or you can search every day as the books that are on sale seem to change pretty often. One great deal I got from the Kindle daily deals was on an investing book I wanted for a while about competitive advantages that normally sold for between $50-$80 that and found on a Kindle daily deal for free.

In my opinion the internet is one of the top three greatest inventions this world has ever seen as it has enabled everyone around the world to be able to learn as much as they want with a lot of the resources being cheap or free. You no longer have to spend tens or hundreds of thousands of dollars to go to a big time university to learn from the same information they do. In a topic like investing where going to a university isn't absolutely necessary you can become even better than them while also saving a lot of time and money as I hope was illustrated throughout this book. The main problem with the internet though is that it is infinite and growing every day. When searching for things of interest about a topic like value investing it is very easy to get lost in the muck and waste a lot of time on useless information. For example a quick search of value investing on Google brings up as of the time of this writing 195 million pages and a search for how to value a company brings up 333 million pages, yikes. This is why it took me nearly five years to get to where I am because of all the wasted time. The goal of this book and the accompanying blog is to talk about and share with you the very best information that I have personally learned from to save you a lot of time, frustration, and to help show you the path to becoming a better value investor faster so that you can potentially start earning money faster.

I hope that I have done a good job of accomplishing those goals.

Epilogue

"Rule number one: never lose money. Rule number two: never forget rule number one." Warren Buffett

I hope you have been able to see the progress that can be made in a short period of time because you can make the same progress if you follow the lessons of this book. When I started to dedicate myself to getting better I tried to learn and implement as many new things as possible into every article as you probably noticed in the huge chapter on Altria. After doing this for a while and getting a bit overwhelmed I decided it would probably be better just concentrating on adding or learning one new thing for each article written I found that this was a much better way for me to do things as I improved much faster than when trying to learn many new things at once. Going by this process I also noticed that my analysis was still concentrated, I was improving more, and the actual analysis articles got much better because I understood what I was doing better than when trying to learn multiple things at once.

The exact process of becoming a better investor is tough and when you first start, you will probably be doing a lot of things and concentrating in areas that you later will have no interest in. Treat every company you research as a potential learning experience, try new things, and continue to constantly push for improvement. Your investing journey will change drastically over time and it is a good thing if it does because it means you are pushing yourself to keep learning and improving.

As an example of how far you can come using the principles and techniques outlined in this book I want to show you how much I was able to improve in just one year once I dedicated myself to becoming an excellent value investor. The following is my first ever stock "analysis" write up. The information is completely unedited other than change of the font, size of font, some of the formatting, and a few typos.

Vodafone Group PLC, ADR, (VOD) info

All information taken from Morningstar.com, Vodafone's website, fool.com, or Vodafone's most recent annual financial report.

Overview:

With 343 million proportional customers (total customers multiplied by its ownership interest), including its 45% stake in Verizon Wireless, Vodafone is the second-largest wireless phone company in the world behind China Mobile. It is also the largest carrier in terms of the number of countries served. Vodafone has majority or joint control in 22 countries and minority or partnership interests in more than 150 total countries. The firm's objective is to be the communications leader across a connected world. They have four major markets that they break their financials into: Europe, Africa Middle East and Asia Pacific or AMAP, India, and the United States through a partnership with Verizon.

Pros:

- Huge company operating in more than 150 countries making them more diversified and able to withstand drops in revenues and profits coming from a single region or country.
- Generates huge free cash flows of at least $8.25 Billion in each of the last 8 financial years. Free cash flow or FCF is basically the money that's left over after expenses, dividends, payments, etc that the Vodafone can use as it pleases. Generally VOD uses their FCF to increase their dividends, buyback their own stock, acquire other companies, or pay down debt.
- Current dividend yield of 6.97%, the average company in the S&P 500 has a yield of around 2%. Pays a semiannual dividend in June and

November of each year. Also receiving a special dividend from Verizon, $1 billion of which will go to paying down Vodafone debt, $3.5 Billion will go to pay a special dividend to Vodafone shareholders in January or February of 2012.
- FCF/Sales ratio over 16% each year since the 2002 financial year. Anything over 5% means they are generating huge amounts of cash.
- Interest coverage ratio of 23.4, anything over 1.5 is good. Interest coverage ratio is how many times they can cover the payments of interest on their debt.
- Payout ratio of around 50% for the dividend meaning the dividend should be safe for the foreseeable future.
- Raising their dividend an average of 7% per year for the next 3 years.
- Lower debt/equity than their industry competitors.
- Growing a lot in Asia, Middle East, India, and parts of Africa. Also still a lot of room to grow in those areas as they are relatively new to them, especially India.
- Paying down debt with FCF.
- Gross margin, net margin, and EBT margin all over 17% which is very good.
- Still a lot of room to grow their revenue through people upgrading to smart phones and paying for data packages which they make more money off of then regular phones.
- Executive pay is linked to how well the company does, and they encourage their executives and directors to own company stock.

Cons:

1. Still a lot of debt even though they are paying it down, around $40 Billion

2. Most of Western Europe except Germany is having huge economic problems which have led to lower sales and profits in those areas.

3. The fear or actuality of another global recession would hurt their sales and profits.

4. Problems at Verizon which VOD owns 45% of would hurt future payments from Verizon to VOD.

5. Most of their revenue is generated in Europe where as above, there are big financial problems.

6. Since they are in so many countries they have to deal with many regulations and sometimes even lawsuits from other governments or companies in those countries.

Final Thoughts:

Overall I feel very good about Vodafone's prospects to be a great investment for the long-term. We are buying them when they are valued at a very good price, especially compared to their competitors. They have huge growth potential in India, a country that has over 1.3 billion people, as they have only penetrated that market by around 10%. They are paying down debt, upping their dividends and receiving a special dividend from Verizon. Even if their share price doesn't go up over the next few years, which I believe it will by quite a bit, then we are still covered by the near 7% dividend that they are going to keep growing at least 7% a year for the next 3 years. Also, with their huge FCF they can maybe pay down debt faster, acquire other companies to keep growing, pay more dividends, or buyback their stock.

As always if there are any questions let me know. I believe we will all do well with this stock in our portfolios over the long-term.

Jason Rivera

Go back and compare this to any of the chapters in the book and the difference is shocking. Shocking in how inadequate my thinking still was at this point where I was investing real money as most of the above you can tell was taken directly from financial sites and the companies own website, not exactly in-depth independent analysis on my part. The reason I put my first ever write-up in this book is to illustrate how much better you can get in a very short time frame by using the principles and techniques outlined in this book and dedicating yourself to constantly improving.

If you do love value investing, have followed what has been shown to you in this book, have read from some of the sources that I have talked about and listed on my blog, and have the drive to continually improve yourself and get better, I guarantee that you will now be better at evaluating whether a company is a potentially fantastic investment better than most MBA's and professional level investors without having to spend tens or hundreds of thousands of dollars at a big time university and saving years of time having to research all of this information for yourself.

Thank you so much for buying this book, good luck, and continue to work constantly at getting better and improving your processes.